In Living *Color*

Also by Daniel R. Hyde

Jesus Loves the Little Children:
Why We Baptize Children

The Good Confession:
An Exploration of the Christian Faith

What to Expect in Reformed Worship:
A Visitors' Guide

Called to Serve:
Essays for Elders and Deacons (contributor)

God With Us:
Knowing the Mystery of Who Jesus Is

With Heart and Mouth:
An Exposition of the Belgic Confession

Daniel R. Hyde

In Living *Color*

Images of Christ and the Means of Grace

Reformed Fellowship, Inc.
3363 Hickory Ridge Ct. SW
Grandville, MI 49418

© 2009 by Daniel R. Hyde
All rights reserved.

Reformed Fellowship, Inc. is a religious and strictly nonprofit organization composed of a group of Christian believers who hold to the biblical Reformed faith. Its purpose is to advocate and propagate this faith, to nurture those who seek to live in obedience to it, to give sharpened expression to it, to stimulate the doctrinal sensitivities of those who profess it, to promote the spiritual welfare and purity of the Reformed churches, and to encourage Christian action.

Requests for permission to quote from this book should be directed to:
Editor, The Reformed Fellowship, 3363 Hickory Ridge Court,
Wyoming, MI 49418.

Unless otherwise indicated, all Scripture quotations are from The Holy Bible, English Standard Version, copyright © 2001 by Crossway Bibles, a division of Good News Publishers. Used by permission.
All rights reserved.

Book design by Jeff Steenholdt.

Printed in the United States of America

ISBN 978-0-9793677-3-1

To all pilgrims
who have not seen Christ
in this age, yet love him,
believe in him, and rejoice
with inexpressible joy,
waiting for their faith to be
turned to sight in the
age to come.

Contents

Foreword

IN POST-MODERN, twenty-first-century Western society, biblically sanctioned and carefully crafted confessional statements of the Reformed faith are either blatantly challenged or simply discarded as irrelevant for the church. *In Living Color* effectively addresses one doctrine that increasingly is being discarded—the scriptural and confessional rejection of man-made images of Christ.

In these pages, Danny Hyde argues with great clarity against all images of Jesus as man-made media. He shows that all such images are abominated in Scripture and roundly rejected by the Reformed confessional heritage without exception. Hyde goes on to argue, however, that God does provide us with His "media"—the preaching of His Word and the administration of His sacraments.

I hope that you, like me, will realize as you finish reading this book how poor man's media are and how rich God's media are! I am grateful for Rev. Hyde's bold and unequivocal stand on this subject. I also believe that this book has far-reaching implications for all of worship. What the Christian church needs today is not more man-made innovations but God's anointed ministers who preach the Word and administer the sacraments with the Spirit's unction. Also needed are God-fearing parishioners who are satisfied with the media of God's provision and, with it, thrive spiritually in worshiping God.

We would do well to heed the wise, pastoral counsel of the images of Christ that *In Living Color* provides. We must be convicted of the sin of allowing the present-day philosophy of our time to please people as much as possible and to become our philosophy of ministry. A true philosophy of ministry is that we aim to please God as much as possible by worshiping Him in a Christ-centered way in accord with His Word.

Above all, may God grant us grace to "look upon Him in the Word and sacraments" with ever greater awe and pleasure, so that we might be changed from glory to glory (2 Cor. 3:18).

Joel R. Beeke
Puritan Reformed Theological Seminary
Grand Rapids, Michigan

Acknowledgements

EVERYTIME I set out to put my thoughts onto pages I am reminded of the generosity and encouragement of the council of pastors, elders, and deacons at the Oceanside United Reformed Church, who allow me "diligently to teach and faithfully to defend" in my public preaching and writing the doctrines of the Reformed confessions in fulfillment of my vows in the Form of Subscription. I wish to thank Henry Gysen, George Knevelbaard, and all the members of the Reformed Fellowship board for their continued kindness in publishing what I write. An entire world of people like me who did not grow up in a Reformed church is out there, and your efforts to provide solid, accessible material introducing them to aspects of our precious Reformed Faith is commended. My heartfelt gratitude also goes out to Jeff Steenholdt and Mindy Wheeler for their painstaking work in designing and typesetting this book. As always, I thank my wife, Karajean, and my sons, Cyprian and Caiden, who are ever so willing to show me the grace and forgiveness of Jesus, not merely in words, but "in living color."

Introduction

GOD AND JESUS—at least their names—have been no strangers to the silver screen. Billed as "the greatest event in motion picture history," Cecil B. DeMille's 1956 Oscar-winning movie, *The Ten Commandments,* portrayed the story of God's acts in redeeming Israel through Moses (Charlton Heston) from the clutches of Egypt and the Pharaoh (Yul Brynner). This movie included God, albeit conservatively imaged as an iridescent flame in the midst of the burning bush. Hollywood's account of Jesus' life hit the big screen almost a decade later in the Oscar-nominated *The Greatest Story Ever Told* (1965) with Max Von Sydow playing Jesus of Nazareth.

With these acclaimed films, it was only a matter of time until American evangelical Christians and Hollywood would unite, becoming strange bedfellows indeed. What Hollywood produced as dramatized art in the mid-twentieth century in the two aforementioned movies has now turned into a means of evangelism in the twenty-first century. With the release of *The Passion of the Christ* in 2004, Hollywood took notice that it could make money—a lot of money, in fact—while evangelicals could make a lot of converts. With the release of *Evan Almighty* in 2007, the modern-day retelling of Noah and the Flood, with Oscar winner Morgan Freeman as God and Golden Globe-winning comedic actor, Steve Carrell as "Noah," modern evangelicalism and Hollywood have come full circle in their partnership. Evangelism by means of entertainment has reached the big time.

That the visual media of television and movies are forms of entertainment has been forcefully argued by no less an authority than New York University communications theorist Neil Postman, who said, "Entertainment is the supra-ideology of all discourse on television. No matter what is depicted or from what point of view, the overarching presumption is that it is there for our amusement and pleasure."[1] The medium of television, and movies, is inevitably entertainment, no matter the intention. This is even true of "religious" television. Postman chronicles that "televangelism" is not outside the influence of the media, but is drastically affected by it.[2] This is why he insightfully concludes, "I believe I am not mistaken in saying that Christianity is a demanding and serious religion. When it is delivered as easy and amusing, *it is another religion altogether*" (emphasis added).[3]

These recent movies and the evangelistic fervor they have created among American evangelical Christians present an excellent opportunity to evaluate the legitimacy of portraying God and Jesus Christ through the medium of visible pictures

and movies, whether as a means of artistic expression, education, entertainment, or ultimately, evangelism.[4]
This growing legitimization of using film as an evangelistic tool creates another opportunity for Reformed Christians in the twenty-first century to *re-evaluate* their historic aversion to portraying any of the three persons of the holy Trinity—Father, Son, and Holy Spirit—especially the incarnate Son, Jesus Christ, in pictures, paintings, stained glass windows, and now movies. I say *re-evaluate their historic aversion to portraying any of the three persons of the holy Trinity* because our forefathers understood the second commandment, "Thou shalt not make unto thee any graven image" (Ex. 20:4; KJV), to forbid images of Jesus Christ. As we will see in this book, they expressed this understanding in the catechisms and confessions they wrote and that the Reformed churches officially adopted as the faith of their churches.

The Struggle of Being in the World but Not of the World

For many Reformed Christians today, this principle of having no images leads to an intense struggle with how the principle is put into practice, especially since our culture today is so image-saturated. Recently, the group TV-Free America compiled statistics showing that 99% of American households have a television, that the average American household has 2.24 televisions, and that 66% of American households have three or more televisions. The result of this is that the television is turned on for an average of six hours and forty-seven minutes a day in American homes.

The struggle for the Reformed Christian comes from the desire to follow Jesus' words, when he said that we were to be in the world as its salt and light (Matt. 5:13–16), but also his words about not being of the world (John 17:6, 11, 13, 16). As salt, we are the preservative of this world, as God withholds his judgment for the sake of saving people out of the world, "from every tribe and language and people and nation" (Rev. 7:9). As light, we are to be a beacon, leading people to the truth in the midst of darkness. How do we do this with our lives and lips? Should we or should we not rely on the world's methods of advertising and entertainment that surround us as a means of getting the Word of God into the homes of lost sinners? We need to be rigorous, then, in our thinking about the theological principle of having no images, the culture around us, and the nexus between the two.

An illustration of this struggle between this Reformed principle of forbidding pictures of Christ and its application in practice was the 2004 movie, *The Passion of the Christ.* Reformed pastors across the land can testify of the intense questions parishioners asked about whether or not we as Reformed believers were allowed to see this movie or not. In my parish, even with a strong sense that we are living as pilgrims in this life, awaiting the "better country" (Heb. 11:16), my parishioners desired to involve their faith in the public sphere since this movie was so visible to the culture and it seemed to be just the opportunity to communicate Christ.

In many Reformed churches across the United States, like my own, the precious heritage of the Reformed church has opened the eyes of many from the man-centered theologies and churches marking the landscape and has brought them to place the glory of God first in their thinking about his amazing grace. Many of these ex-evangelical Christians who had become Reformed in their theology and life saw *The Passion of the Christ* as an opportunity to keep up their commitment to witnessing and evangelism with their neighbors. After all, this would also be an opportunity to show our evangelical brothers and sisters that we do care about evangelism, despite being known as "the frozen chosen." As Reformed Christians, we do believe in the church's mandate to fulfill the Great Commission (Matt. 28:18–20) by preaching the gospel "promiscuously and without distinction" (Canons of Dort, II.5) and we have a desire to make Christ known far and wide.[6] We pray earnestly and daily that God will use the gospel to turn many to saving faith in Jesus. The question for the Christian whose beliefs and life are reformed according to the Word of God, though, is not *whether* to bear witness to our unsaved neighbors and support the work of evangelism, but *how* we do this.

The Passion of the Christ generated an enormous amount of interest and emotion in both the church and the world.

As those who believe in the sovereignty of God, confessing our faith week by week publicly that we believe in "God the Father almighty, Maker of heaven and earth" in the Apostles' Creed, we do not deny that God is able to use this movie or any other means to some good end. For us, however, that is not the point. Just because God *can* do something does not mean he *will.* In other words, the question is not what God may or may not do in any given situation, but how he has promised to work. This question he answers in his revealed Word. Here we follow Deuteronomy 29:29, which distinguishes between the things revealed in God's Word and the things hidden from us: "The secret things belong to the Lord our God, but the things that are revealed belong to us and to our children forever, that we may do all the words of this law." This verse applies to the question at hand in the following way. God may use a movie about Jesus to convert the lost; after all, he is God. This is hidden from us, though. We simply do not know if he will use a movie or not. What we need to do is think about and speakof God in the way he wants us to, taking his revealed Word seriously and seeking to apply it to our time and place in history. In a word, we must attempt to be a people who are faithful to the Scriptures since they are God's revealed will to us.[7]

In the context of *The Passion of the Christ* and its promotion as "perhaps the best outreach opportunity in 2000 years," I counseled my congregation to ask the question, what has God revealed to us in Scripture about the way we are to do the work of evangelism?[8] My counsel was not intended to dampen my parishioners' evangelistic zeal, but to redirect that zeal by explaining why the historic, confessionally Reformed position forbids making or using any images of any of the three persons of the glorious triune God—including the incarnate Son, Jesus Christ—and to focus our evangelistic zeal towards living holy lives before the world, being prepared to give an answer to those who may ask us about our hope (1 Pet. 3:15), to pray for the lost, and to invite them to hear the preached Word of the gospel.

A Struggle that No Longer Exists?

According to some, though, this struggle between principle and practice, reformation and relevance, no longer exists, or at least that it should not exist in the mind of the Reformed Christian. One example was a recent article on the *Christianity Today* website, in which G. Jeffrey MacDonald wrote an article entitled, "Reformed Protestants No Longer See Images as Idolatrous."[9] In it, he said, "Reformed Protestants no longer see images as idolatrous…a longstanding hallmark of Reformed tradition is disappearing." This was not really surprising, given the sad state of Christianity in the United States in our day.

What was surprising, though, was the effort MacDonald took in attempting to demonstrate his thesis of a "new Reformation" occurring among churches with Reformed roots and his tacit assumption that if the churches he cited as evidence thought images were permitted, then we can assume all "Reformed" churches agreed. While realizing that the evidence Mr. MacDonald adduced and the conclusions of his findings are fairly well entrenched across the landscape of American Protestantism, there is another point of view. It is not quite a lone "voice in the wilderness," but at least it is a voice from "the other side of the tracks." It is a voice that needs to be heard to continue the conversation. This voice is the historic Reformed position on the second commandment, which this book will seek to exposit and apply.

The Meaning of "Reformed"

Of course all that I am saying implies that there is a difference in being an evangelical Christian, at least in its American connotation, and a *Reformed* Christian. In order to explain this more fully we will think about the meaning of that word "Reformed" here. To do this, we will continue to use G. Jeffrey MacDonald's article as the background of our considerations, since he gives expression to commonly held beliefs about the meaning of the word Reformed. In his article, MacDonald's argument exhibits several fundamental flaws, which evidence a certain predisposition to his thesis that "Reformed" churches are no longer against images of Christ in the various forms of art—paintings, icons, statues, windows, and movies.

First, the article does not demonstrate a working knowledge of what the title "Reformed" actually stood for in the sixteenth century or what it continues to stand for by those who self-consciously define themselves by it. The reader gets the impression that the only significance in being Reformed in a historical sense is that the sixteenth-century Reformers could not stand good works of art! MacDonald's article leads one to think that Reformed Christians rallied around the banner, "Down with Michelangelo! Down with Rembrandt!" Furthermore, one is left thinking that being a Reformed Christian today means belonging to a generic mass of evangelical churches, except for having remote roots in at least a branch of the Reformed tradition.

To be "Reformed" means so much more than simply being tied to some obsolete tradition. No mention was made in MacDonald's article that to be a part of a Reformed church means to be reformed according to Scripture. The Protestant reformers confessed the great doctrine of Scripture alone (*sola Scriptura*), which is the sufficient source for Christian belief, life, and worship. Because of this emphasis on getting back to the source of divine truth in the Scriptures, the Reformers proclaimed passionately that sinners are justified before the judicial bar of an almighty and holy God by faith alone (*sola fide*) in Christ alone (*solus Christus*). These twin truths of Scripture and faith, *sola Scriptura* and *sola fide*, were codified in the Reformation catechisms and confessions such as the Three

Forms of Unity—the Belgic Confession (1561), Heidelberg Catechism (1563), and Canons of Dort (1618–19)—and the Westminster Standards—the Westminster Confession of Faith and Larger and Shorter Catechisms (1647).

This is so important for our day, in which we are seeing many come to the Reformation faith, life, and worship from the mass of evangelical churches dotting our land. We certainly rejoice in this, but must also be aware that for many of these zealous Calvinists, to be Reformed means that they have come to learn about the so-called "five points of Calvinism," or, as it is better described, "the doctrines of grace." Many think that *this* is Reformed theology.

To have a "Reformed theology" means so much more than believing in the acronym TULIP. To be Reformed means to be confessional. This means that we confess the Bible as the Word of God alone and as it is summarized faithfully for us in the ancient Christian creeds of the church and in the Reformation catechisms and confessions mentioned above. These documents define for Reformed churches who they are and why they are who they are.

A cursory glance at the Belgic Confession of Faith, published in 1561, for example, reveals that to be Reformed is not only to believe in the sovereignty of God in salvation, but also the following:

- That God exists and reveals himself through creation generally, and Scripture especially (arts. 1–2);

- That the sixty-six books of the Old and New Testaments alone are the Word of God (arts. 3–7);
- That God is a triune God as the ancient churches and creeds declare (arts. 8–11);
- That God made all things out of nothing (art. 12);
- That the God who made everything also cares for everything (art. 13);
- That humanity has been plunged into hopelessness by Adam's sin (arts. 14–15);
- That God's grace alone provides the remedy in Jesus Christ (arts. 16–17);
- That Jesus Christ is one person in whom are united two distinct natures, a divine nature and a human nature as the ancient Definition of Chalcedon teaches (arts. 18–19);
- That by faith alone in Christ alone we are justified our sins are forgiven and Christ's righteousness is imputed to us (arts. 20–23);
- That we are sanctified by the power of the Holy Spirit (art. 24);

- That having been brought into union with Christ through faith alone we are brought into union with Christ's church as its members (arts. 27–28);
- That there are true churches and false churches, and that true churches have three "marks": the pure preaching of the gospel, the pure administration of the sacraments, and the exercise of church discipline (art. 29);
- That this church is ruled according to a presbyterian form of church government where all ministers are equal and where congregations have a role to play in the calling of church officers (arts. 30–31);
- That worship is to be enjoyed and performed according to the "regulative principle of worship" (art. 32);
- That baptism and the Lord's Supper are means of grace (art. 33);
- That the children of believers are members of the covenant and therefore are to be baptized (art. 34);
- That there is a "real presence" of Christ in the Lord's Supper (art. 35);
- That Jesus Christ has already begun to reign and that he shall come again once, at the end of the ages, to judge the living and the dead (art. 37).[10]

These very confessions that define our theology, life, and worship include the prohibition against images of God and of Jesus Christ, as we shall see in the next chapter.

The second flaw of MacDonald's article under question is the problem of selective evidence. Mentioned among "Reformed" institutions and denominations are Andover Newton Theological School, whose faculty is made up of ministers/elders in the United Church of Christ, Disciples of Christ, American Baptist, United Methodist, and Presbyterian Church (U.S.A.). He also provides quotations from a minister at "Warehouse 242," which is affiliated with the Evangelical Presbyterian Church, a minister at "Hope Church," which is a joint effort of both the United Church of Christ and the Disciples of Christ, and a professor at Calvin College, which is the college of the Christian Reformed Church, which was recently excluded from the North American Presbyterian and Reformed Council (NAPARC) in 2002.[11] Add to this the unsubstantiated claim that "Reformed" missionaries are no longer relying on Bibles, but on the "Jesus Film" to do their work.

To be charitable, I will include all the institutions/denominations just mentioned under the "Reformed" umbrella. In doing so, it is no stretch to say that these are on the left of the theological spectrum. The selectivity of evidence is shown in the fact that no quotations or citations were given from ministers/professors from any of the North American Presbyterian and Reformed Council (NAPARC) churches on

our continent. Surely it is not too hard to find someone from the Presbyterian Church in America, Heritage Reformed Churches, Associate Reformed Presbyterian Church, Reformed Presbyterian Church in North America, Free Reformed Churches, or United Reformed Churches in North America, to name a few.
The question of whether "Reformed" Protestants no longer see images as idolatrous remains to be answered by MacDonald's essay.

Add to this the fact that Mr. Macdonald's thesis is propped up with the emotionally repulsive story of Calvinists running through towns like madmen, destroying beautiful art. This may have been true in some instances, such as in the Netherlands in the 1560's when religious and political zeal united against the tyranny of Phillip II of Spain, yet one need only read the most recent research on the history of the Netherlands in the 1550s–60s to understand the context in which this was done, as well as the fact that many of the Reformed preachers were against this wave of iconoclasm.[12] MacDonald also uses the imagery of "whitewashing" churches, which comes from the history of the Reformed churches in Zürich under the leadership of Ulrich Zwingli. What he does not mentioned was the fact that images (idols, and not simply artistic Christian expression) were removed decently and in an orderly way by order of the city council in June 1524. He also does not mention the fact that St. Pierre's Cathedral in Geneva, where John Calvin preached, had a cross atop its spire that was not over-zealously removed. When it was struck by lightning and it caught on fire, it was not replaced.[13]

When Mr. MacDonald says that the Reformed tradition "has for centuries regarded pictures with great suspicion," it depends on what kind of pictures he is speaking about; if those of Christ and/or the Father and Spirit, then absolutely, yes. This is not to equate religious images of the holy Trinity with art, though. This is incorrect. It is not art that the Reformers responded to, but to the false religion fostered by stained glass windows, statues, and crucifixes. In Reformed terminology an "image" refers to any representation of any of the persons of the Holy Trinity (Westminster Larger Catechism, Q&A 109; Heidelberg Catechism, Q&A 96–98), not to artistic expression of God's creation.

Conclusion: The Purpose of this Book

Contrary to MacDonald's article, then, not all Reformed Protestants agree that Christian's have the freedom to use images of Jesus Christ, nor do they agree with his overstatement that this point of view is disappearing. After all, we are not simply voicing crass iconoclasm or outmoded tradition, but we are expressing a position firmly rooted in biblical exegesis, the Protestant confessions, and church history.

The simple purpose of the book you hold in your hands, then, is to give a pastoral explanation from Scripture and our confessions for the classic Reformed prohibition of images of God and Jesus Christ from Scripture and our confessions. We will do this by looking at man's desire for the visual in his relationship with God, but then we will show how God rejects man's efforts to image him. Instead of images, God has given the new covenant church the Word and sacraments as manifestations of his presence among us until Christ comes again, visibly and corporeally—in living color.

1 Man's Media: *Images*

Thou shalt not make unto thee any graven image, or any likeness of any thing that is in heaven above, or that is in the earth beneath, or that is in the water under the earth. Thou shalt not bow down thyself to them, nor serve them.

—Exodus 20:4–5a (KJV)

Man's nature, so to speak, is a perpetual factory of idols.

—John Calvin[1]

Calvin's argument is that there is no such thing as an "innocent" religious image. Their acceptance alone is an act of idolatry, so that as soon as images appear, religion is corrupted and adulterated.

—Carlos M. N. Eire[2]

GOD CREATED US to be multi-sensory creatures, with the ability to hear, taste, touch, smell, and see. Our eyes and the ability to see are gifts from God that he declared "very good" in the beginning (Gen. 1:31). Concerning the eyes, Solomon wisely wrote, "The hearing ear and the seeing eye, the LORD has made them both" (Prov. 20:12). After Moses debated with the LORD about his qualifications for service, the LORD said to Moses, "Who has made man's mouth? Who makes him mute, or deaf, or seeing, or blind? Is it not I, the LORD? (Ex. 4:11) The Psalmist reinforced that sight is a gift of God, asking rhetorically of the "dullest of the people": "He who formed the eye, does he not see?" He asked this because the enemies of God were arrogantly boasting, persecuting the LORD's people, and killing widows, sojourners, and orphans, all the while saying, "The LORD does not see; the God of Jacob does not perceive" (Ps. 94:1–9).

Of course we live in a fallen world that is affected so tragically by Adam's sin. One such tragedy is that not all can see. Yet, at least one of those who were blind during the life of our Lord was so because he would be a means of revealing the glory of God and the identity of Jesus Christ as Messiah.

> As he passed by, he saw a man blind from birth.
> And his disciples asked him, "Rabbi, who sinned,
> this man or his parents, that he was born blind?"
> Jesus answered, "It was not that this man sinned,
> or his parents, but that the works of God might be

> displayed in him . . . They brought to the Pharisees the man who had formerly been blind. Now it was a Sabbath day when Jesus made the mud and opened his eyes. Some of the Pharisees said, "This man is not from God, for he does not keep the Sabbath." But others said, "How can a man who is a sinner do such signs?" And there was a division among them . . . So for the second time they called the man who had been blind and said to him, "Give glory to God. We know that this man is a sinner." He answered, "Whether he is a sinner I do not know. One thing I do know, that though I was blind, now I see." And they reviled him, saying, "You are his disciple, but we are disciples of Moses. We know that God has spoken to Moses, but as for this man, we do not know where he comes from." The man answered, "Why, this is an amazing thing! You do not know where he comes from, and yet he opened my eyes. We know that God does not listen to sinners, but if anyone is a worshiper of God and does his will, God listens to him. Never since the world began has it been heard that anyone opened the eyes of a man born blind. If this man were not from God, he could do nothing" (John 9:1–3, 13–14, 16, 24–25, 28–33).

The hope of all God's children, whether they can see or not in this life, is that every aspect of the curse will be removed from their lives in the life to come so that "they will see his face" (Rev. 22:4).

Seeing God—what theologians call the "beatific vision" (*visio beatifica*)—is an even more amazing thing than our LORD did for the man born blind. Sight in this age and the hope of seeing God in the person of Jesus Christ in the age to come are God-given gifts.

The Desire for the Visual

With this aspect of our human nature in mind, what is so interesting about the narrative of Scripture is that from the beginning Satan has tempted us through this God-given sense of sight. This is one of Satan's "schemes" (*methodeias;* Eph. 6:11) as he takes what God has given us and twists it to his own perverted end. What God gives out of his goodness, Satan seeks to use and turn into the cause of God's judgment upon those whom he created.

Genesis 3

We see this strategy in the Garden of Eden. The LORD God gave his law to the first man, saying, "You may surely eat of every tree of the garden, but of the tree of the knowledge of good and evil you shall not eat, for in the day that you eat of it you shall surely die" (Gen. 2:16–17). The LORD God was so generous and liberal in his provision to Adam. He only forbade him to eat of one tree. Even this law was meant to be a "delight" for our first father, Adam, to meditate upon "day and night" (Ps. 1:2), because in his created state, he was "good, righteous, holy, [and] capable in all things to will agreeably to the will of God" (Belgic Confession, art. 14).[3] When the serpent entered the Garden, he twisted this law, questioning the Lord God's authority, promising instead that if our first parents ate of the tree of the knowledge of good and evil, "Your eyes will be opened, and you will be like God"(*immah*; Gen. 3:6). In his conversation with Eve, while Adam stood idly by, being "with her" (Gen. 3:6), Satan quickly moved from the Word that God spoke, which Adam and his wife heard, to the things they could see. The result of the serpent's promise was that "the woman *saw* (*ra'ah*) that the tree was *good* (*tov*) for food, and that it was a delight to the eyes," therefore "she *took* (*laqah*) of its fruit" (Gen. 3:6). Their sin, transgressing the law of God because they rebelled against the LORD God's authority over them in order to become "like God" (Gen. 3:5), came through tempting the eyes of Adam's wife.

Genesis 5

Soon thereafter, in the early history of the antediluvian world, we read of the sin of the sons of God in Genesis 6. What is so intriguing about the way Moses described their sin was that he used the same terms that he used to describe the sin of the first man and woman: "The sons of God *saw* (*ra'ah*) that the daughters of man were *attractive* (*tovot*). And they *took* (*laqah*) as their wives any they chose "(Gen. 6:2). Whether these "sons of God" were the godly line of Seth who intermarried with the ungodly line of Cain, the "daughters of man,"[4] or they were kingly rulers whose title was "sons of God" and who showed their authority in taking from "daughters of man" wives, of "any they chose,"[5] the point is the same: their sin was a result of the lust of the eye.

Exodus 32

After the LORD led Israel out of Egypt and through the Red Sea on dry land, he brought them to the foot of Mount Sinai to ratify his covenant relationship with them. While there, the Israelites grew weary of Moses' being on the mountain in the presence of the LORD for so long, while they were below. Therefore, they went to Aaron and demanded a visible god: "Up, make us gods who shall go before us. As for this Moses, the man who brought us up out of the land of Egypt, we do not know what has become of him" (Ex. 32:1). In his commentary on this verse, John Calvin explained that the LORD provided an abundance of visual demonstrations of his presence:

> Moreover, although God offered Himself as if present with them by day and by night in the pillar of fire, and in the cloud, they still despised so illustrious and lively an image of His glory and power, and desire to have Him represented to them in the shape of a dead idol . . . Could they not see the pillar of fire and the cloud? Was not God's paternal solicitude abundantly conspicuous every day in the manna? Was he not near them in ways innumerable?[6]

Calvin then explained the root of the Israelites' problem was idolatry—the creating of images based in human imagination and opinion:

> Yet, accounting as nothing all these true, and sure, and manifest tokens of God's presence, they desire to have a figure which may satisfy their vanity. And this was the original source of idolatry, that men supposed that they could not otherwise possess God, unless by subjecting Him to their own imagination. Nothing, however, can be more preposterous; for since the minds of men and all their senses sink far below the loftiness of God, when they try to bring Him down to the measure of their own weak capacity, they travesty Him. In a word, whatever man's reason conceives of Him is mere falsehood; and nevertheless, this depraved longing can hardly be repressed, so fiercely does it burst out. They are also influenced by pride and presumption, when they do not hesitate to drag down His glory as it were from heaven, and to subject it to earthly elements. We now understand what motive chiefly impelled the Israelites to this madness in demanding that a figure of God should be set before them, viz., because they measured Him by their own senses . . . Nevertheless, however they may deceive themselves under this or that pretext, they still desire to be creators of God.[7]

What is so revealing about this story is that so soon after the Israelites responded to the giving of the law of the covenant, "All that the LORD has spoken, we will do, and we will be obedient" (Ex. 24:7), they desired what was in violation of the second commandment. The result was a golden calf, which Aaron did not proclaim was another god, but the God of Israel, saying, "These are your gods, O Israel, who brought you up out of the land of Egypt . . . Tomorrow shall be a feast to the LORD" (Ex. 32:4, 5). Even worshipping the true God in a way that God has not required, especially in a visible way, caused the LORD's "wrath [to] burn hot against them [that] I may consume them" (Ex. 34:10).

Numbers 21/2 Kings 18

Soon after, as they wandered around the land of Edom, the Israelites "became impatient on the way" and "spoke against God and against Moses, 'Why have you brought us up out of Egypt to die in the wilderness? For there is no food and no water, and we loathe this worthless food'" (Num. 21:4–5). The memorable story ensued of the LORD's judgment in sending "fiery serpents" to bite and even kill some of the Israelites and of the Lord's salvation in commanding Moses to "make a fiery serpent and set it on a pole, and everyone who is bitten, when he sees it, shall live" (Num. 21:8). As Christians we easily associate our Lord's words about himself with this story of the bronze serpent: "As Moses lifted up the serpent in the wilderness, so must the Son of Man be lifted up, that whoever believes in him may have eternal life" (John 3:14–15). What we do not so easily recall is that this bronze serpent reappears between the time of Moses' creation of it and our Lord's sermon about it. Several hundred years after Moses, in the days when the kingdoms of Judah and Israel were divided, the LORD raised up king Hezekiah over Judah to reform its worship. Hezekiah "did what was right in the eyes of the LORD (2 Kings 18:3), which meant that, "he removed the high places and broke the pillars and cut down the Asherah" (2 Kings 18:4). Most importantly, "he broke in pieces the bronze serpent that Moses had made." Why would he do such a thing to something the LORD had commanded to be made? The story goes on to say, "For until those days the people of Israel had made offerings to it (it was called Nehushtan)" (2 Kings 18:4). Once more Satan used a good gift of God as an opportunity to lead the people of God astray into idolatry. Their desire for the tangible and the visual led them to worship the bronze serpent as if it were their god.

John 20

As we move from the Old Testament to the New Testament and the climax of redemptive history, we recall that the Son of God who became man "was crucified, dead, and buried; he descended into hell; the third day he rose again from the dead" (Apostles' Creed). Even after all of this we see humanity's desire for the visual in the example of Thomas. Not being content with the disciples' words about the resurrection of the Lord, "doubting" Thomas demanded a visible demonstration that the Lord Jesus was alive: "Unless I see in his hands the mark of the nails, and place my finger into the mark of the nails, and place my hand into his side, I will never believe" (John 20:25). After all, seeing is believing, as the saying goes.

Romans 1

This desire within all of us to see the unseen God has been manifested among the nations of the earth for millennia in the form of idolatry. Idolatry is "instead of the one true God who has revealed himself in his Word, or along with the same, to conceive or have something else on which to place our trust" (Heidelberg Catechism, Q&A 95).[8] Any idea or actual representation that we put in the place of God, or even alongside the true God, is idolatry. This sin of idolatry is a universal human phenomenon after the fall of Adam. It is the reason the apostle Paul could say,

> For what can be known about God is plain to them, because God has shown it to them. For his invisible attributes, namely, his eternal power and divine nature, have been clearly perceived, ever since the creation of the world, in the things that have been made. So they are without excuse. For although they knew God, they did not honor him as God or give thanks to him, but they became futile in their thinking, and their foolish hearts were darkened. Claiming to be wise, they became fools,

> and exchanged the glory of the immortal God for images resembling mortal man and birds and animals and reptiles. Therefore God gave them up in the lusts of their hearts to impurity, to the dishonoring of their bodies among themselves, because they exchanged the truth about God for a lie and worshiped and served the creature rather than the Creator, who is blessed forever! Amen (Rom. 1:19–25).

As we have seen, it is a precious gift to be able to see the things God has made, taking delight in the beauty of creation all around us. The clarity of creation in revealing the existence and attributes of God is seen in the Psalmist's poetic personification of the creation as a preacher when he said, "The heavens declare the glory of God, and the sky above proclaims his handiwork. Day to day pours out speech, and night to night reveals knowledge. There is no speech, nor are there words, whose voice is not heard" (Ps. 19:1–3). Unfortunately, because of our first parents' willingness to follow the serpent's temptation, and because of the result of that sin, we are all too eager to turn God's good gifts into the means of making our sinful desires a reality. Thus humanity has perpetually "exchanged the glory of the immortal God for images resembling mortal man and birds and animals and reptiles . . . exchang[ing] the truth about God for a lie and worship[ing] and serv[ing] the creature rather than the Creator, who is blessed forever! Amen" (Rom. 1:23, 25).

Summary

This desire within our minds to conceive and create with our hands images of the Divine is an inherited part of our sin nature. This is why John Calvin said the root of the idolatry in Genesis 3 and 6, Exodus 24, Numbers 21, and Romans 1 was "that man tries to express in his work the sort of God he has inwardly conceived. Therefore the mind begets an idol; the hand gives it birth."[9] This sin nature is also manifested in the culture we build with our hands. As Neil Postman has masterfully shown in his book, *Amusing Ourselves to Death*, our idolatry for the visual is perverting what was once a word-based culture into an image-based culture, wherein our ability to think, learn, and communicate is weakened. In reflecting on the second commandment, Postman calls us to pause and ponder its application for our broader society, saying,

> The God of the Jews was to exist in the Word and through the Word, an unprecedented conception requiring the highest order of abstract thinking. Iconography thus became blasphemy so that a new kind of God could enter a culture. People like ourselves who are in the process of converting their culture from word-centered to image-centered might profit by reflecting on this Mosaic injunction.[10]

It is to this injunction in the second commandment and otherer biblical injunctions that we now turn.

Biblical Teaching Against Images

We desire images. This is the medium our sinful hearts want. I hope that is clear from the foregoing section. As we now turn to meditating upon the LORD's second commandment and its associated texts and biblical teachings, we will profit immensely since the Bible's teaching so clearly prohibits humanity from creating images as the medium through which we catch a glimpse of God.

Second Commandment

In bringing the Israelites out of a land of idols in Egypt and preparing them to enter a land of idols in Canaan, the LORD spoke the second of his "Ten Commandments," literally, his "ten words" (*aseret ha-divarim*; Deut. 4:13, 10:4). In the traditional rendering of this passage we read:

> Thou shalt not make unto thee any graven image, or any likeness of any thing that is in heaven above, or that is in the earth beneath, or that is in the water under the earth. Thou shalt not bow down thyself to them, nor serve them: for I the LORD thy God am a jealous God, visiting the iniquity of the fathers upon the children unto the third and fourth generation of them that hate me; and shewing mercy unto thousands of them that love me, and keep my commandments (Ex. 20:4–6 cf. Deut. 5:8–10; KJV).

Here the Lord defines the reason for prohibiting the making and serving of images in the fact that he is a "jealous" God. This jealousy is not to be understood in its connotation as envy and treating people and things as objects to hoard, but as Michael Horton has recently shown, "God's jealousy is his zeal. Like a devoted spouse of parent, God is passionately committed to his covenant."[11] This means that he is passionate about who he is, about us as his people, and for defining the terms on which we may relate to him. We must remember, he is the Creator and we are the creatures; therefore, it is his right to dictate whom to worship as well as the what, when, where, and why of his worship. In a word, because God is jealous for us, we are to be jealous for him.

The second commandment's opening prohibition is clear: "Thou shalt not make unto thee any graven image." The LORD's forbidding the creating of images was reiterated throughout the Old Covenant law. Several examples suffice to show that this commandment was central to the life of the church under Moses:

> You shall not make gods of silver to be with me, nor shall you make for yourselves gods of gold (Ex. 20:23).
>
> Do not turn to idols or make for yourselves any gods of cast metal: I am the LORD your God (Lev. 19:4).
>
> You shall not make idols for yourselves or erect an image or pillar, and you shall not set up a figured stone

> in your land to bow down to it, for I am the LORD your God (Lev. 26:1).

In fact, the Israelites were to be so zealous for this prohibition that they were to go on an iconoclastic crusade against the idols of the land they were soon to enter by not even repeating the names of their neighbors' gods as well as destroying their idols:

> Be careful to do everything I have said to you. Do not invoke the names of other gods; do not let them be heard on your lips (Ex. 23:13).
>
> You shall tear down their altars and break their pillars and cut down their Asherim (Ex. 34:13).
>
> . . . then you shall drive out all the inhabitants of the land from before you and destroy all their figured stones and destroy all their metal images and demolish all their high places (Num. 33:52).
>
> You shall tear down their altars and dash in pieces their pillars and burn their Asherim with fire. You shall chop down the carved images of their gods and destroy their name out of that place (Deut. 12:3 cf. 7:5).

Deuteronomy 4

When the people of Israel were at the end of their forty years of wandering in the wilderness, Moses delivered to them the law of the covenant LORD a second time in the book of Deuteronomy. Just before Moses recited the Ten Commandments, the LORD spoke powerfully through Moses, saying,

> *Your eyes have seen* what the LORD did at Baal-peor, for the LORD your God destroyed from among you all the men who followed the Baal of Peor . . . Only take care, and keep your soul diligently, lest you forget the things that *your eyes have seen,* and lest they depart from your heart all the days of your life. Make them known to your children and your children's children—how on the day that you stood before the LORD your God at Horeb, the LORD said to me, "Gather the people to me, *that I may let them hear my words,* so that they may learn to fear me all the days that they live on the earth, and that they may teach their children so" . . . *You heard the sound of words, but saw no form; there was only a voice . . .* Therefore watch yourselves very carefully. Since *you saw no form* on the day that the LORD spoke to you at Horeb out of the midst of the fire, beware lest you act corruptly by making a carved image for yourselves, in the form of any figure, the likeness of male or female, the likeness of any animal that is on the earth, the likeness of any winged bird that flies in the air, the likeness of anything that creeps on the ground, the likeness of any fish that is in the water under the earth. And beware lest you raise your eyes to heaven, *and when you see* the sun and the

> moon and the stars, all the host of heaven, you be drawn away and bow down to them and serve them, things that the LORD your God has allotted to all the peoples under the whole heaven . . . Take care, lest you forget the covenant of the LORD your God, which he made with you, and make a carved image, the form of anything that the LORD your God has forbidden you. For the LORD your God is a consuming fire, a jealous God. When you father children and children's children, and have grown old in the land, if you act corruptly by making a carved image in the form of anything, and by doing what is evil in the sight of the LORD your God, so as to provoke him to anger, I call heaven and earth to witness against you today, that you will soon utterly perish from the land that you are going over the Jordan to possess . . . And the LORD will scatter you among the peoples, and you will be left few in number among the nations where the LORD will drive you. And there you will serve gods of wood and stone, the work of human hands, that neither see, nor hear, nor eat, nor smell (Deut. 4:3, 9–10, 12, 15–19, 23–26a, 27–28; emphasis added).

Here Moses says the Israelites saw the LORD executing his judgment against those whose sexual lust caused them to join the Moabite women in sacrificing to Baal, the god of the land of Canaan (Num. 25), but they did not see the LORD on

Mount Horeb. Instead, they only heard his voice. It was because they saw no form of God on the mountain that they were not to make any carved forms of anything to worship the LORD through or instead of him. In fact, if they did create images of God, he would exile them to the nations that practiced such worship to give them their fill of images! One overlooked aspect of this narrative is that the generation Moses addresses either was not at the mountain, since they were too young at the time of the address, or, they were too young to remember. As Moses recounts that they saw the LORD's works in redeeming and judging and did not see his form on the mountain but heard his voice, he speaks to the later generation as if they were there because they are a part of the covenant people of God.[12]

Of note in Deuteronomy 4 is that the Lord reminded this next generation of the children of Israel that they "saw no form" (v. 12, 15) of God, but only heard his word. Historically, Reformed theologians have used this text to support their interpretation that we must not make any images of God because the Israelites saw no form. Recently, however, David VanDrunen of Westminster Seminary California has challenged the validity of this text as a proof for this position.[13] Of this text, VanDrunen says, "Deuteronomy 4:15 does not teach that God *has* no form—as the traditional argument seems to understand it—but that the people *saw* no form, and those two things are not necessarily the same."[14] VanDrunen concludes his discussion of this text, saying it does prohibit images:

> . . . not absolutely, however, but only until God stoops to become visible in revelation . . . Of course, one of the great confessions of the Christian faith is that God *has* stooped to become visible through revelation, in the Incarnation of the Son.[15]

Although the LORD hid himself from the Israelites in the Old Testament, he did reveal himself in visible and tangible ways through theophanies, that is, visible manifestations of himself in things like the smoking fire pot with Abram (Gen. 15:17), the burning bush with Moses (Ex. 3), the pillar of cloud and fire with the Israelites in the exodus (Ex. 13:17ff.), the thunder, lightning, cloud, and trumpet sound at Sinai (Ex. 19), and the LORD's glorious presence between the wings of the cherubim on the ark of the covenant within the Holy of holies in the tabernacle (Ex. 25:22). Yet all these "incarnations" of the LORD were types and shadows of the incarnation of the Son of God in human flesh in the Lord Jesus Christ.

Psalm 115

Moving forward in the Canon of Scripture, we come to the Psalms. The Psalter was the concrete expression of the people's response to the LORD's covenant faithfulness in song and prayer. In Psalm 115, the people of God sang of the LORD in contrast to the idle idol of the nations:

> Not to us, O LORD, not to us,
> but to your name give glory,
> for the sake of your steadfast love

and your faithfulness!
Why should the nations say,
"Where is their God?"
Our God is in the heavens;
he does all that he pleases.
Their idols are silver and gold,
the work of human hands.
They have mouths, but do not speak;
eyes, but do not see.
They have ears, but do not hear;
noses, but do not smell.
They have hands, but do not feel;
feet, but do not walk;
and they do not make a sound in their throat. (v. 1–7)

Interestingly, while the nations were saying, "Where is your God?" since Israel had no images of him, the people sang of him "who art in heaven." Although the nations were full of images, their gods were impotent, being unable to speak, see, hear, smell, feel, or walk. In contrast, the LORD was able to do that which he pleased.

Isaiah

Of course we know how Israel's history turned out. They were exiled from the land "east of Eden" because of their disobedience in creating and serving idols. The prophets' critiques and denunciations of Israel's idolatry and the impending judgment from the hand of the LORD are too numerous to recount in full. Isaiah opens his book of prophecy by addressing the people of God as children whom the LORD "reared and brought up, but [who] have rebelled against me" (1:2). Although "the ox knows its owner, and the donkey its master's crib . . . Israel does not know, my people do not understand" (1:3). He continued, calling God's people a "sinful nation," "laden with iniquity," an "offspring of evildoers," and, "children who deal corruptly" (1:4). Most damning was addressing them as Sodom and Gomorrah" (1:10). The reason for Isaiah's strong language was that "their land [was] filled with idols; they bow down to the work of their hands, to what their own fingers have made" (2:8). Later, in his "book of comfort" (chs. 40–66), Isaiah denounces the people of God, saying,

> To whom then will you liken God,
> or what likeness compare with him?
> An idol! A craftsman casts it,
> and a goldsmith overlays it with gold
> and casts for it silver chains.
> He who is too impoverished for an offering
> chooses wood that will not rot;
> he seeks out a skillful craftsman
> to set up an idol that will not move (40:18–20).

The prophet continued to denounce idolatry in sarcastic terms, making fun of the idle idols that had to be created by men's hands, weighed on scales, carried over the shoulders, and that could not speak or save:

> To whom will you liken me and make me equal,
> and compare me, that we may be alike?
> Those who lavish gold from the purse,
> and weigh out silver in the scales,
> hire a goldsmith, and he makes it into a god;
> then they fall down and worship
> They lift it to their shoulders, they carry it,
> they set it in its place, and it stands there;
> it cannot move from its place.
> If one cries to it, it does not answer
> or save him from his trouble (46:5 7).

This line of argument was similar to the ancient secular poet Horace, who spoke sarcastically of this practice, saying, "Once I was a little fig tree trunk, a useless bit of wood, when the workman, in doubt whether he should make a stool, preferred that I be a god."[16] These texts comparing the glory of the Lord to the idols of the nations led John Calvin to say,

> God's glory is corrupted by an impious falsehood whenever any form is attached to him . . . every statue man erects, or every image he paints to represent God, simply displeases God as something dishonorable to his majesty.[17]

Jeremiah

Because of the fact that the LORD's glory belonged to him alone, images necessarily took away from his glory and placed it in the creativity of man. For this reason, the weeping prophet Jeremiah, in sarcastic tones reminiscent of Isaiah, said so vehemently,

> Hear the word that the LORD speaks to you,
> O house of Israel. Thus says the LORD:
> Learn not the way of the nations,
> nor be dismayed at the signs of the heavens
> because the nations are dismayed at them,
> for the customs of the peoples are vanity.
> A tree from the forest is cut down
> and worked with an axe by the hands of a craftsman.
> They decorate it with silver and gold;
> they fasten it with hammer and nails
> so that it cannot move.
> Their idols are like scarecrows in a cucumber field,
> and they cannot speak;
> they have to be carried,
> for they cannot walk.
> Do not be afraid of them,
> for they cannot do evil,
> neither is it in them to do good (Jer. 10:1–5).

Acts 17

Paul spoke in prophet-like terms when he addressed the Athenian philosophers in the Areopagus, saying,

> So Paul, standing in the midst of the Areopagus, said: "Men of Athens, I perceive that in every way you are very religious. For as I passed along and observed the objects of your worship, I found also an altar with this inscription, 'To the unknown god.' What therefore you worship as unknown, this I proclaim to you. The God who made the world and everything in it, being Lord of heaven and earth, does not live in temples made by man, nor is he served by human hands, as though he needed anything, since he himself gives to all mankind life and breath and everything . . . Being then God's offspring, we ought not to think that the divine being is like gold or silver or stone, an image formed by the art and imagination of man (Acts 17:22–25, 29).

In the context of Graeco-Roman religion, with its temples for the gods and visible representations of the gods in statue-idols, Paul spoke of God as one not dwelling in temples and not being served through idols of men's making. Furthermore, Paul argued that because the "divine being" was not like gold, silver, or stone, he could not be represented in visible art or even in the human imagination. This idea that God could not be imaged by the art and imagination of men was an ancient argument used by the philosophers, although merely to reform and not abolish the practice of the ancient Graeco-Roman society.[18] The ancient church fathers, though, drew upon these pagan philosophers, but to forbid images absolutely. One example of this was the Council of Elvira (ca. 300–306), which said in its thirty-sixth canon: “There should be no pictures in church, lest what is reverenced and adored be painted on walls.”[19] In his article on this canon, Robert Grigg details the scholarly interpretations and historical background of this language from the ancient Synod before offering an alternative interpretation:

> What they seem to have feared, by their own testimony, was the act of painting that which is reverenced and adored upon walls. They did not simply fear that images of God or Christ might be worshiped, as if one could distinguish between a proper and improper use of such images. Their fear was evidently based upon a more fundamental consideration. The very act of circumscribing divinity by painting it on walls was a self-evident sacrilege. It was an insult to God, who had no need of such images.[20]

Not only did the prophets sarcastically show the folly of making idols, and not only did the apostle Paul and later the Synod of Elvira say it was impossible to make images of God, but Paul roots images in man’s imagination, not God’s revelation.

Responding to an Advocate of Images

Paul's words here in Acts 17:29, therefore, are a powerful response to the position taken recently by Jeffrey J. Meyers. In an essay, Meyers says that if the argument against images of Jesus Christ is based on the fact that they are all inaccurate and based in the imagination of man, this would mean all art was wrong.[21] This does not follow, though, since God gave us our imaginations, but not to image him according to "human imagination." Yet, Meyers says, no artist claims his picture of Christ is actually what Christ looked like, but is the result of the artists' imagination "*to artistically and imaginatively abstract these qualities for us by portraying them on canvas so as to enhance our understanding and appreciation of the event*" (emphasis in original).[22] In fact, Meyers says this is why every culture needs to image Christ according to their cultural features.[23] This is precisely the issue Paul rebukes in Acts 17:29, though, when he speaks of images "formed by the art and imagination of man." Finally, Meyers claims that the position that images of Christ are forbidden because they are based on the imagination of man is a philosophical argument, not a biblical one.[24] Once more, the apostle Paul's sermon on Mars Hill lays this objection to rest. John Murray echoed Paul's invocation of the idea that human imagination is the root of images when he said,

> A picture of Christ, if it serves any useful purpose, must evoke some thought or feeling respecting him and, in view of what he is, this thought or feeling will be worshipful. We cannot avoid making the picture a medium of worship. But since the materials for this medium of worship are not derived from the only revelation we possess respecting Jesus, namely, Scripture, the worship is constrained by a creation of the human mind that has no revelatory warrant. This is will-worship.[25]

Summary

Because of these reasons, Paul would later say in his letter to the Romans that although the Gentiles claimed "to be wise," in fact "they became fools" because they "exchanged the glory of the immortal God for images resembling mortal man and birds and animals and reptiles" (Rom. 1:22–23). They who prided themselves on truth and knowledge "exchanged the truth about God for a lie and worshiped and served the creature rather than the Creator, who is blessed forever! Amen" (Rom. 1:25).

To sum up all these biblical passages that teach us about the nature of God and that prohibit idolatry, we can turn to the end of St. John's first epistle. There he exhorts his readers, and us: "Little children, keep yourselves from idols. Amen" (1 John 5:21).

The Incarnation

Let us move from the particular texts cited above to the second reason Scripture forbids the making of images—the nature of the incarnation of the Son of God. When we move from the Old Testament, where the LORD said the Israelites saw no form of him on the mountain, and enter the New Testament, things change dramatically. The curtain of the drama of God's redemptive plan was lifted. That unseen form of the Son of God, who "was in the form of God" (Phil. 2:6), became visible in the person of Jesus Christ. Whereas God spoke "long ago, at many times and in many places to our fathers by the prophets" (Heb. 1:1), he has "in these last days spoken to us by his Son" (Heb. 1:2). He no longer speaks to us through the veils of prophets and mediators since he came and spoke to us "face to face" (2 Cor. 4:6 cf. Ex. 33:11; Deut. 5:4, 34:10; Judg. 6:22). Thus John records with startling words that the Word, that is, the eternal, personal wisdom of God, who "was with God" and who "was God" (John 1:1), "became flesh and dwelt among us" (John 1:14). In the incarnation, that is, in the Son of God becoming a man, "we have seen his [the Father's] glory." That glorious fire on Mt. Sinai (Ex. 20), that glory between the cherubim's wings (Ex. 25:22), that glory which filled the temple in Isaiah's vision (Isa. 6), made its home in our humanity. John's terminology in John 1:14 can literally be translated, "And the Word became flesh and *tabernacled* among us." The eternal God became subject to time; he who was invisible became visible; he who was infinite became finite; he who was immutable became mutable! This is why Paul says of the Son, "He is the image (*eikōn*) of the invisible God" (Col. 1:15).

In Jesus Christ the Son of God took human form, and thus Paul could say "in him the whole fullness of deity dwells bodily" (Col. 2:9). He was a real, true, authentic human being just like you and me, "yet without sin" (Heb. 4:15). This means that he took to himself a true body and a true soul, with all that this entails in terms of physical features, personality, emotions, and everything that makes us what we are.[26] One of the great Reformation confessions of faith, the Belgic Confession expresses the reality of the incarnation and the necessity of it, saying that the Son of God "did not only assume human nature as to the body, but also a true human soul, that he might be a real man. For since the soul was lost as well as the body, it was necessary that he should take both upon him, to save both."[27]

The reality of the incarnation is the reason we cannot create any image of Jesus Christ in any form. This is in contrast to Eastern Orthodox[28] and Lutheran claims that the incarnation of the Son is the reason we are able to create icons or images. Even some Reformed Christians utilize this argument.
The Reformed filmmaker, Brian Godawa, made the following comment in his review of The Passion of the Christ in response to the standard Reformed objections to the movie:

> . . . it is sufficient to note that any understanding of the second commandment must do justice to the fact of the incarnation of God in the Person of Jesus of Nazareth. Moses' statement in Deuteronomy 4:15, offered as the ground of the second commandment, "you saw no form of any kind the day the LORD spoke to you at Horeb out of the fire. Therefore watch yourselves very carefully," can no longer be said of the incarnate God. It is true, we have no physical "portraiture" of Christ (and any such attempts must be acknowledged as imaginative), but that Jesus can be portrayed dramatically as a human being in historical situations does not seem counter to the concerns of the second commandment. As Greg L. Bahnsen reminded us, we dare not allow our interpretation of the second commandment to lead us into a docetic diminution of the reality of the incarnation. The Passion of the Christ is a narrative depiction of Christ's humanity and His fulfillment of His mission as "the Lamb of God who takes away the sin of the world" (John 1:29), not an iconic representation of His divinity to worship.[29]

Well-known Reformed theologian, John Frame, also argues in favor of depicting Jesus Christ based on the incarnation. He argues that because God has become flesh and since his disciples saw him, touched him, and lived among him (cf. 1 John 1:1–3), we can therefore make images of him.[30]

The concern of Godawa, Frame, the Orthodox, and Lutheran Christians is that we do not believe Jesus only "appeared" (Greek, *dokein*) to be human, but in fact was truly human as well as divine. This is a commendable starting point. As David VanDrunen has recently written, we can affirm with *iconophiles* (icon-lovers)/*iconodules* (icon-servers), that it would have been possible ontologically for all who saw the Word made flesh to have made an image of him as with any other person because they saw him. For this reason, the exegesis of John 12:20–21 by Peter Barnes in his book, *Seeing Jesus,* is lacking. Barnes says that when the Greeks asked, "Sir, we wish to see Jesus," Jesus did not show an image, but preached to them. This exegesis seeks to prove too much from this text. After all, it was Jesus who *was before them as he preached.*[31]

While Jesus was seen and could be remembered by those who saw him during his ministry on earth, for the generations of those who have not seen him it is impossible to create an image of Jesus. As we will see below, our place in redemptive history does not allow us to make any representation of Jesus Christ because this is the age of not seeing him (1 Peter 1:8). Even more simply, the fact is that we do not know what he looked like. Because we believe in a real incarnation we believe that Jesus Christ had distinctive features as a distinct human being. Any image of "Jesus Christ," then, according to VanDrunen, "is authentic only as it attempts to represent Christ's actual appearance."[32] The reason is that Jesus

> . . . was a certain height and weight, his hair and eyes certain colors, his skin a particular pigmentation. His nose and mouth had a form unique to him . . . God can only be seen, and therefore portrayed, in Jesus Christ, and Jesus Christ was not generic humanity with general feature, but a particular human being with specific features.[33]

This argument against images of Jesus from the reality of the incarnation is a traditional argument Reformed theologians have used for centuries. Most recently, it was the main case the aforementioned Peter Barnes made, when he said,

> Since God is spirit (John 4:24) and hence invisible (1 Timothy 1:17), a physical representation of Him is impossible . . . the point remains: Christ has come in the flesh, but we have no real idea what he looked like. The Holy Spirit has not told us whether Christ was short or tall, solid or slender, with blue eyes or brown, dark hair or fair; such things are not numbered among those needed to make us "wise unto salvation." It is thus incontestable that all pictures of Christ are inaccurate and that we have no way of knowing how accurate."[34]

This argument has been a concern of Reformed interpreters in the past. For example, in 1753 the three founders of the Associate Presbytery in Scotland, James Fisher, Ralph Erskine, and Ebenezer Erskine, wrote what is called Fisher's Catechism.

Fisher's Catechism is an exposition of the Westminster Shorter Catechism. The Shorter Catechism, Q&A 51, asks, "What is forbidden in the second commandment?" It goes on to answer, saying, "The second commandment forbiddeth the worshiping of God by images, or any other way not appointed in his Word."[35]

Fisher's Catechism explains Westminster Shorter Catechism, Q&A 51, with several of its own questions and answers, including:

> Q. 10. Why ought all pictures of Christ to be abominated by Christians?
>
> A. Because they are downright lies, representing no more than the picture of a mere man: whereas, the true Christ is God-man; "Immanuel, God with us," 1 Tim. 3:16; Matt. 1:23.[36]

Images of Jesus represent "a mere man," that is, a generic representation of an artist's mind and not the "one mediator between God and men, the man Christ Jesus" (1 Tim. 2:5). Another eloquent use of this argument can be found in the work of the American Presbyterian, Loraine Boettner (1901–90), who wrote:

> But nowhere in the Bible, in either the Old or New Testament, is there a description of Christ's physical features. No picture of Him was painted during His earthly ministry. The church had no pictures of Him during the first four centuries. The so-called pictures of Christ, like those of Mary and the saints, are merely the

> product of the artist's imagination. That is why there are so many different ones. It is simply an untruth to say that any one of them is a picture of Christ. All that we know about His physical features is that He was of Jewish nationality. Yet He more often is represented as having light features, even as an Aryan with golden hair. How would you like it if someone who had never seen you and who knew nothing at all about your physical features, resorted to his imagination and, drawing on the features of his own nationality, painted a picture and told everyone that it was a picture of you? Such a picture would be fraudulent.[37]

Boettner gives three arguments from the reality of the incarnation. First, there is no biblical description of Jesus Christ. Second, there are no images of him from the most ancient period of the church. Third, any such picture, then, is based on imagination, not revelation. This is no Reformed philosophical argument, either, as biblical studies also confirm this argument. In an article by Edward M. Curtis, he argues that images of the LORD were forbidden, not only because they were prohibited by the second commandment, but also because they were not actual images of the LORD; therefore, by definition these images were other gods:

> Neither the prophets nor the historiographers clearly distinguish between the violation of the first and second commandments. Perhaps this reflects the fact that much

> of the idolatry practiced in Israel and Judah resulted from the influence of foreigners with whom Israel came in contact and thus would involve the use of images. Perhaps it reflects the idea that an image of Yahweh would not be Yahweh, and any worship of a Yahweh image was then by definition the worship of other gods. For the Biblical authors the fact was that Yahweh could not be worshiped by means of an image. The pragmatic reality was that the worship of other gods involved the use of images, and the worship of images (even an image of Yahweh) was the worship of other gods.[38]

One such example of what Curtis is saying is from the story of Jeroboam, in the latter half of 1 Kings 12. His kingship was characterized by consolidating power through the means of false worship. His reasoning was that if the people obeyed the LORD by going to Jerusalem to sacrifice, they would end up becoming loyal to his rival, Rehoboam. His solution was to build two golden calves (not one, as Aaron did) and to make a decree: "Behold your gods, O Israel, who brought you up out of the land of Egypt" (12:28). Jeroboam's reasoning could also be seen as religious reformation, since, after all, it was Solomon who introduced the worship of false gods while Jeroboam was calling Israel back to worshipping the LORD who redeemed them. Yet, while Jeroboam created idols to depict the LORD, the LORD himself viewed these as other gods: "but you have done evil above all who were before you and have gone and made for yourself *other gods* and metal images, provoking *me* to anger, and have cast *me* behind your back" (1 Kings 14:9; emphasis added).

The result, therefore, of any representation is what the inspired and authoritative apostle called "an image formed by the art and imagination of man" (Acts 17:29).[39] Because the Lord Jesus Christ is a real man, our imagination is the only way we could ever make an image of a person we call "Jesus Christ," although whomever we imaged would not be the Jesus who was born, walked this earth, ascended into heaven, and that will return to take us to himself.

Our "Living Hope"

The final piece of the biblical puzzle is eschatology, as alluded to above. While the Son descended and became incarnate as our Lord Jesus Christ, he also ascended back to heaven. Because of his ascension, as Christians we live in an age between his two advents—the first, to inaugurate redemption, and the second, to consummate redemption. The apostle Paul describes the Christian's hope for the resurrection of the body and of all things, saying, "For in this hope we were saved. Now hope that is seen is not hope. For who hopes for what he sees? But if we hope for what we do not see, we wait for it with patience" (Rom. 8:24–25). Our eschatology creates in us the experiential virtues of hope, as we long for Christ's coming to complete what he began in us, and patience, as we are content to live in this age.

This eschatological hope of seeing the Lord Jesus is expressed in the New Testament in no better way than by the apostle Peter. As the one who denied our Lord three times before the crucifixion (John 18:15–18), only to live in despair until Jesus restored him after the resurrection (John 21:15–19), no one knew about hope more than Peter. Peter wrote to Christians who live between the resurrection and second coming, saying, "Though you have not seen him, you love him. Though you do not now see him, you believe in him and rejoice with joy that is inexpressible and filled with glory" (1 Peter 1:8). In 1 Peter the apostle describes the life of the "elect exiles" (1:1). All throughout this epistle he describes us as pilgrims (1:1, 17, 2:11, 4:2), being like the Israelites as they wandered in the wilderness, outside the Promised Land, having been redeemed but not yet fully experiencing the blessings of that redemption. He writes to congregations filled with believers who had never seen the Lord, yet who believed in him nonetheless. He wrote to those who were the fruit of our Lord's promise to Thomas, when he said, "Have you believed because you have seen me? Blessed are those who have not seen and yet have believed" (John 20:29). This situation in which we love and believe in him apart from seeing him is a temporary one: "Though you do not *now* see him." This will cease when the Lord appears or we go to be with him after death.

Seeing God in the face of Jesus Christ is one of the blessings of that consummate redemption for which we hope. It is what ancient Christian theologians called the "beatific vision" (*visio beatifica*). It was also the hope of the saints in both the Old and New Testaments:

> For the LORD is righteous;
> he loves righteous deeds;
> the upright shall behold his face (Ps. 11:7).
>
> As for me, I shall behold your face in righteousness;
> when I awake, I shall be satisfied with your likeness (Ps. 17:15).
>
> One thing have I asked of the LORD,
> that will I seek after:
> that I may dwell in the house of the LORD
> all the days of my life,
> to gaze upon the beauty of the LORD
> and to inquire in his temple (Ps. 27:4).
>
> Blessed are the pure in heart, for they shall see God (Matt. 5:8).
>
> . . . so Christ, having been offered once to bear the sins of many, will appear a second time, not to deal with sin but to save those who are eagerly waiting for him (Heb. 9:28).
>
> Strive for peace with everyone, and for the holiness without which no one will see the Lord (Heb. 12:14).

> Beloved, we are God's children now, and what we will be has not yet appeared; but we know that when he appears we shall be like him, because we shall see him as he is (1 John 3:2).

On that day, what we do not see, we shall embrace. The moving words of John are our hope: "They will see his face" (Rev. 22:4). *But not yet!* Now we hope. Now we pray. Now "we walk by faith, not by sight" (2 Cor. 5:7). Now we long to see him. Notice that there is tension between the way things are *now,* and the way things will be *then.* As John says,

> Beloved, we are God's children *now,* and *what we will be* has not yet appeared; but we know that *when* he appears *we will be* like him, because *we shall see* him as he is. And everyone who thus *hopes* in him purifies himself as he is pure (1 John 3:2–3; emphasis added).

The Christian life is about hoping for what we will receive, or, rather, who will receive us! The beatific vision is that most blessed vision of God that we do not see—*yet!* Paul says this in this way: "For now we see in a mirror dimly, *but then* face to face" (1 Cor. 13:12).

The "blessed hope," this "beatific vision," is to see our Husband, to whom we are now engaged (an arranged marriage if you will), on the day of consummation. This age between Christ's two advents is the age of faith, of hope, and of love. This is why in historic Christian and Reformation worship services we exclaim in the dialog before the Lord's

Supper, "Lift up your hearts! We lift them up to the Lord!"[40] We long for our Husband-to-be; we look for him; we desire him; we ache for him. This is why Jesus said, "A little while, and you will see me no longer; and again a little while, and you will see me" (John 16:16). VanDrunen spoke of this passage and its implications for images, saying, "The age of the Spirit is an age of Christ's presence, to be sure, but an age of his invisible presence, to be followed by his reappearance."[41] For this reason, the hopeful, patient, pilgrim people of God must not "move the eschatological clock ahead of schedule."[42]

Confessional Teaching Against Images

As we said in the introduction, to be Reformed is to be confessional. As Protestants we confess the Word of God alone as the source and final standard for our faith, life, and worship. Because the Word alone is that authoratative source and rule, our Protestant and Reformed forefathers summarized its teachings in the confessions and catechisms of the Reformation in order to testify to the Roman Catholic Church and to the world what the Reformed churches believed. On the issue of pictures of Jesus Christ, all of the Reformed catechisms and confessions of faith reject all images of Christ. Because of this, the confessions are the best response to the previously mentioned essay by Jeffrey J. Meyers. In his essay, Meyers argues for what he calls a limited use of images of Christ in art and education, not worship, whether private or public.[43] One of his arguments is that we do not have a long list of writings going back to the Reformation on the issue of the rejection of images:

> Has the Reformed church really rejected artistic and illustrative pictures of Jesus? If it has, where are published theological and biblical apologies for this viewpoint? Why don't we have such a train of published works stretching back to the Reformation?[44]

This list of rhetorical questions begs the question because whether or not individual Reformed theologians wrote about their rejection of images is moot. The Reformed churches, as churches, have spoken in their confessions and catechisms and have rejected images. This was not a private position of a few reformers, then, but was and remains the official position of the churches that were Reformed according to the Word of God. The following survey will bear this out.

Heidelberg Catechism (1563)

Published in 1563 under the direction of Frederick III, one of the seven electors of the Holy Roman Empire, who ruled the region of Germany known as the Palatinate, the Heidelberg Catechism is "the most widely used and most warmly praised catechism of the Reformation period"[45] because of its biblical and devotional quality. In its exposition of the second commandment, three questions are asked and answered.[46] In question 96, we are asked,

> Q. What does God require in the second commandment?
>
> A. That we in nowise make any image of God, nor worship him in any other way than he has commanded in his Word.[47]

What is so important about the answer given is that it understands the requirements of the second commandment to be twofold: first, we may not make *any* images of God, and second, we may not worship him except how he has commanded in his Word. This exposition of the command comes from the text of Scripture itself, which gives prohibitions against making images (*lo ta'aseh*) and against worshipping them (*lo tishetaheveh/lo ta'abedem*). These words become the foundation of the classic Reformed interpretation of the command, exemplified by John Calvin:

> Now we must remark, that there are two parts in the Commandment—the *first* forbids the erection of a graven image, or any likeness; the *second* prohibits the transferring of the worship which God claims for Himself alone, to any of these phantoms or delusive shows. Therefore, to devise any image of God, is in itself impious; because by this corruption His Majesty is adulterated, and He is figured to be other than he is. There is no need of refuting the foolish fancy of some, that all sculptures and pictures are here condemned by Moses, for he had no other object than to rescue God's glory from all the imaginations which tend to corrupt it.[48]

The seventeenth century Genevan theologian, Francis Turretin (1623–87), advanced this interpretation that the second commandment has two aspects. In his *magnum opus*, he exposited these two aspects when he said:

> Whether not only the worship but also the formation and use of religious images in sacred places is prohibited by the second commandment? We affirm against the Lutherans.
>
> We do not condemn historical representations of events or of great men, either symbolical . . . or political . . . But here we treat of sacred and religious images which are supposed to contribute something to the excitation of religious feeling. . . .God expressly forbids this in the second commandment, where two things are prohibited—both the making of images for worship and the worshipping of them. . . . Therefore to make images to worship them are not to be regarded in the second commandment only a means and end, but as two parts of the divine prohibition.[49]

Question and answer 97 of the Heidelberg Catechism reiterates this point, making sure we understand the purpose of the second commandment. It does so with the common objection, that if we cannot make images, then may we make an image of anything?

> Q. Must we, then, not make any image at all?
>
> A. God may not and can not be imaged in any way;
> as for creatures, though they may indeed be imaged,
> yet God forbids the making or keeping any likeness
> of them, either to worship them, or by them to
> serve himself.

When question and answer 96 said that we must "in nowise make any image of God," this is explained further in question and answer 97, which says, "*God* may not and can not be imaged in any way." We may not make an image of God, and even if we wanted to, we could not do this, since it is implied that God is spiritual.[50] Question and answer 96 also said we are not to "worship him in any other way than he has commanded in his Word." Since we cannot make images of the Creator, may we make images of his creation? Question and answer 97 says, "creatures . . . may indeed be imaged." The command is not meant to restrict all painting, drawings, sculpture, and photography, as the common caricature of the Reformed position is stated. What it restricts are images of God absolutely for whatever reason as well as any other image of creation as an object of worship ("either to worship them") or as a means of worship ("or by them to serve himself"). This was also the understanding of Zacharius Ursinus in his Smaller Catechism, Q&A 85, which forbids those images "which are for the purpose of representing or worshipping God."[51] In his Larger Catechism he asked in Q. 165, "Are all sculpted and painted images whatsoever forbidden by this law?" The answer was then given, "No, only those that are made for the purpose of portraying or worshipping God."[52] We do not worship images or worship God through icons, as is the case with the Eastern Orthodox Church.

Images for the purpose of worship are clearly forbidden. The Catechism also distinguishes carefully and wisely artistic images of creation (not the Creator) from their use in worship. Calvin also used this distinction to refute those who taught that the second commandment forbade all images:

> And yet I am not gripped by the superstition of thinking absolutely no images permissible. But because sculpture and painting are gifts of God, I seek a pure and legitimate use of each.[53]

Finally, what about the issue of pictures, paintings, statues, sculptures, icons, or any other use of these media for educational purposes? To this, Q&A 98 turns:

> Q. But may not images be tolerated in churches as books for the laity?
>
> A. No; for we should not be wiser than God, who will not have his people taught by dumb idols, but by the lively preaching of his Word.

The idea that the Roman Catholic leadership used to justify images on the basis of their being "books for the laity" came from the father of the medieval church, Gregory I (the Great). In his two letters to Serenus, Bishop of Marseilles, he praised Serenus for his zeal against image worship, but rebuked him for destroying the images in the churches, since they were valuable to teach the ignorant. In his first letter on this subject to Serenus, he said,

> Furthermore we notify to you that it has come to our ears that your Fraternity, seeing certain adorers of images, broke and threw down these same images in Churches. And we commend you indeed for your zeal against anything made with hands being an object of adoration; but we signify to you that you ought not to have broken these images. For pictorial representation is made use of in Churches for this reason; that *such as are ignorant of letters may at least read by looking at the walls what they cannot read in books.* Your Fraternity therefore should have both preserved the images and prohibited the people from adoration of them, to the end that both *those who are ignorant of letters might have wherewith to gather a knowledge of the history,* and that the people might by no means sin by adoration of a pictorial representation (emphasis added).[54]

Apparently Serenus did not take Gregory's first letter to heart, as a second letter was sent, with even harsher tones, yet with the same pastoral concern for the ignorant to learn through images:

> For indeed it had been reported to us that, inflamed with inconsiderate zeal, thou hadst broken images of

> saints, as though under the plea that they ought not to be adored. And indeed in that thou forbadest them to be adored, we altogether praise thee; but we blame thee for having broken them. . . . For to adore a picture is one thing, *but to learn through the story of a picture what is to be adored is another.* For what writing presents to readers, this *a picture presents to the unlearned who behold, since in it even the ignorant see what they ought to follow; in it the illiterate read.* Hence, and *chiefly to the nations, a picture is instead of reading.* . . . And then, with regard to *the pictorial representations which had been made for the edification of an unlearned people in order that, though ignorant of letters, they might by turning their eyes to the story itself learn what had been done,* it must be added that, because thou hadst seen these come to be adored, thou hadst been so moved as to order them to be broken. . . . And explain to them that it was not the sight itself of the story which the picture was hanging to attest that displeased thee, but the adoration which had been improperly paid to the pictures. . . . And if any one should wish to make images, by no means prohibit him, but by all means forbid the adoration of images.[55]

In contrast to Gregory's desire to use images as educational aids and their history in the Roman Catholic Church, as "books for the laity" the Heidelberg Catechism forbids them, along with artistic expressions of God and images for the purpose of public or private worship. This educational use of images was later rejected by the Dutch Reformed theologian, Wilhelmus a'Brakel (1635–1711), who said,

> Are men permitted to make images of God—that is, of the Father, Son or the Holy Spirit? We declare that the making of images of the Trinity is absolutely forbidden . . . it is vanity to make an image and say that is Christ. We may not honor Christ . . . in this manner. Objection . . . the images of God are of educational value . . . Answer: God has nevertheless forbidden this. This is pagan thinking and we should not pretend it to be beneficial, since it is forbidden.[56]

This official rejection of images for the purpose of education by the Heidelberg Catechism makes one of Brian Godawa's and Jeffrey Meyers' objections moot. They attempt to make the case that rejecting pictures for education would in fact lead to grave results with our children. If our children never see a picture of Jesus as a human, they may be led to become Docetists, that is, unwitting adherents to the ancient heresy that said Jesus only *appeared* to be a man.[57] In fact, Meyers asserts that pictures of Jesus are the *guarantee* of the full humanity of Christ![58] On the contrary, the incarnation itself guarantees the full humanity of the Son of God with or without our imaginative descriptions of him.[59] Besides, our children have learned Heidelberg Catechism, question and answers 96–98, as well as confessed the true humanity of Christ in questions and answers 35 and 47–48 as well as Belgic Confession, articles 18–19, without images for 450 years. Our churches will continue to do the same in the future as well because we are biblical churches, creedal churches, and confessional churches.

Second Helvetic Confession

Shortly after the Heidelberg Catechism was published, Heinrich Bullinger (1504–75) of Zurich published the Second Helvetic Confession in 1566. Originally a private confession of his faith, written in 1561, it was distributed publicly and has had a long history as a treasured expression of the Reformation faith. In chapter 4, entitled, "Of Idols; or of Images of God, of Christ, and of Saints," Bullinger wrote an extensive refutation of images. It begins,

> And because God is an invisible Spirit, and an incomprehensible Essence, he can not, therefore, by any art or image be expressed. For which cause we fear not, with the Scripture, to term the images of God mere lies.[60]

It is impossible to portray God, whether in artistic displays or religious images, because he is spiritual. To the question of whether this applied to the incarnate Son of God, Jesus Christ, Bullinger continued:

> We do therefore reject not only the idols of the Gentiles, but also the images of Christians. For although Christ took upon him man's nature, yet he did not therefore take it that he might set forth a pattern for carvers and painters. He denied that he came 'to destroy the law and the prophets' (Matt. v.17), but images are forbidden in the law and the prophets (Deut. iv.15; Isa. xliv.9). He denied that his bodily presence would profit the Church, but promised that he would by his Spirit be present with us forever (John xvi.7; 2 Cor. v.5). Who would, then, believe that the shadow or picture of his body doth any whit benefit the godly? And seeing that he abideth in us by the Spirit, 'we are therefore the temples of God' (1 Cor. iii.16); but 'what agreement hath the temple of God with idols?' (2 Cor. vi.16).[61]

Bullinger's argument is a basic logical deduction: since the Old Testament forbade images of God, and Jesus did not come to abolish the Old Testament, therefore images are still forbidden. Besides this, Bullinger says, nowhere did Jesus set a pattern for artists to image him in any way. Instead of images, Bullinger said:

> But that men might be instructed in religion and put in mind of heavenly things and of their own salvation the Lord commanded to preach the Gospel (Mark xvi.15)—not to paint and instruct the laity by pictures; he also instituted sacraments, but he nowhere appointed images.[62]

As we can see, the Second Helvetic says what the Heidelberg Catechism also says: we reject images of God and Christ no matter if the purpose is for worship, art, or education. These clear statements show that Meyers' claim that Calvin and the Puritans seldom, if even at all, rejected images of Christ for art and education is misleading.[63] As we will see in chapters two and three, God commands his people to be instructed by the Word and sacraments. If we want to see God, not only are we to be content with these means of grace, but according to Bullinger:

> Furthermore, in every place which way soever we turn our eyes, we may see the lively and true creatures of God, which if they be marked, as is meet, they do much more effectually move the beholder than all the images or vain, unmovable, rotten, and dead pictures of all men whatsoever; of which the prophet spake truly, 'They have eyes, and see not,' etc. (Ps. cxv.5).[64]

Bullinger's final paragraph gave brief testimonies from the ancient church concerning the forbidding of images of God and Jesus Christ:

> Therefore we approve the judgment of Lactantius, an ancient writer, who says, "Undoubtedly there is no religion where there is a picture." And we affirm that the blessed bishop Epiphanius did well, who, finding on the church-doors a veil, that had painted on it the picture, as it might be, of Christ or some saint or other, he cut

> and took it away; for that, contrary to the authority of the Scriptures, he had seen the picture of a man to hang in the Church of Christ: and therefore he charged that from henceforth no such veils, which were contrary to religion, should be hung up in the Church of Christ, but that rather such scruple should be taken away which was unworthy of the Church of Christ and all faithful people. Moreover, we approve this sentence of St. Augustine, 'Let not the worship of men's works be a religion unto us; for the workmen themselves that make such things are better, whom yet we ought not to worship' (*De Vera Religione,* cap. 55).[65]

Bullinger recounts the story of Epiphanius in the Second Helvetic Confession, which was a standard piece of evidence the Reformers used in polemics against Roman Catholics and Lutherans. Epiphanius was the bishop of Salamis in Cyprus, who wrote a letter to John, the bishop of Jerusalem, in 394. At his request, Jerome translated the letter into Latin. In his letter to John, Epiphanius said,

> Moreover, I have heard that certain persons have this grievance against me: When I accompanied you to the holy place called Bethel, there to join you in celebrating the Collect, after the use of the Church, I came to a villa called Anablatha and, as I was passing, saw a lamp burning there. Asking what place it was, and learning it

> to be a church, I went in to pray, and found there a curtain hanging on the doors of the said church, dyed and embroidered. It bore an image either of Christ or of one of the saints; I do not rightly remember whose the image was. Seeing this, and being loth that an image of a man should be hung up in Christ's church contrary to the teaching of the Scriptures, I tore it asunder and advised the custodians of the place to use it as a winding sheet for some poor person. They, however, murmured, and said that if I made up my mind to tear it, it was only fair that I should give them another curtain in its place. As soon as I heard this, I promised that I would give one, and said that I would send it at once. Since then there has been some little delay, due to the fact that I have been seeking a curtain of the best quality to give to them instead of the former one, and thought it right to send to Cyprus for one. I have now sent the best that I could find, and I beg that you will order the presbyter of the place to take the curtain which I have sent from the hands of the Reader, and that you will afterwards give directions that curtains of the other sort—opposed as they are to our religion—shall not be hung up in any church of Christ.[66]

Of note is that Epiphanius not only was zealous to remove a large curtain with what he thought was an image of Jesus Christ, ordered it to be sold and used to aid the poor while replacing it with a plain curtain. Certainly this is a pastoral strategy to follow in our day with stained glass windows or any other representations in our places of worship.

We could also add other testimonies from the ancient church to Bullinger's. For example, writing towards the end of the second century, Irenaeus of Lyons commented on the doctrines of Carpocrates, a Gnostic. The Gnostics were those who followed ancient Greek philosophy in teaching that matter was inherently evil while spirit was good. Therefore, for God to become a man was the greatest offense of all. In his own words, Irenaeus wrote that pictures of Jesus Christ were a peculiarity of the Gnostics of his time:

> Others of them employ outward marks, branding their disciples inside the lobe of the right ear. From among these also arose Marcellina, who came to Rome under [the episcopate of] Anicetus, and, holding these doctrines, she led multitudes astray. They style themselves Gnostics. They also possess images, some of them painted, and others formed from different kinds of material; while they maintain that a likeness of Christ was made by Pilate at that time when Jesus lived among them. They crown these images, and set them up along with the images of the philosophers of the world that is to say, with the images of Pythagoras, and Plato, and Aristotle, and the rest. They have also other modes of honouring these images, after the same manner of the Gentiles.[67]

Westminster Larger Catechism (1648)

Moving ahead several decades and across the English Channel, we come to the Westminster Larger Catechism's exposition of the second commandment. This Q&A is quite possibly the most comprehensive on the topic of images in all the Reformation catechisms and confessions.

> Q. 109. What are the sins forbidden in the second commandment?
>
> A. The sins forbidden in the second commandment are, all devising, counselling, commanding, using, and any wise approving, any religious worship not instituted by God himself; tolerating a false religion; the making any representation of God, of all or of any of the three persons, either inwardly in our mind, or outwardly in any kind of image or likeness of any creature whatsoever; all worshipping of it, or God in it or by it; the making of any representation of feigned deities, and all worship of them, or service belonging to them, all superstitious devices, corrupting the worship of God, adding to it, or taking from it, whether invented and taken up of ourselves, or received by tradition from others, though under the title of antiquity, custom, devotion, good intent, or any other pretense whatsoever; Simony; sacrilege; all neglect, contempt, hindering, and opposing the worship and ordinances which God hath appointed.[68]

Among other things, this Q&A teaches that the second commandment forbids three things: 1) false worship of the true God in a way not commanded in his Word (cf. HC 96), 2) the making of any representation of God (cf. HC 96), whether inwardly or outwardly,[69] and 3) worshipping any representation as God or worshipping him by means of them (cf. HC 97). The second point above is explicated by the Larger Catechism, when it forbids "the making any representation of God, *of all or of any of the three persons*." This clearly includes the person of our Lord, who is both God and man. For whatever reason, Jeffrey Meyers does not see this, but says the Westminster Standards have no explicit condemnation of artistic representations of Jesus Christ.[70] He supports this by appealing to a four-page essay by Donald Weilersbacher, who responds to Larger Catechism, Q&A 109:

> Now if the Catechism merely teaches that we are forbidden to worship a mental image of the Second Person of the Godhead or to bow down before a statue of Jesus which portrays His true humanity, then well and good. But if the intent is to say that we may not have a mental image of what Jesus was like at His birth or crucifixion, or that there may be absolutely no visible representations of Jesus in His humanity, then such an interpretation goes beyond the scope of Scripture (emphasis in original).[71]

The reasons for Weilersbacher's assertion are that we convey mental images of Christ's crucifixion when we preach, that if Jesus had begun his ministry in 1973 there would have been pictures of him, and that the official RPCNA interpretation of Larger Catechism, Q&A 109, was unknown at the time of his writing. The Catechism is clear in its intent, though, as each separate sin is signified grammatically by a semi-colon:

> [1] . . . any religious worship not instituted by God himself; [2] tolerating a false religion; [3] the making any representation of God, of all or of any of the three persons, either inwardly in our mind, or outwardly in any kind of image or likeness of any creature whatsoever; [4] all worshipping of it, or God in it or by it; [5] the making of any representation of feigned deities . . .

Summary

What we learn from all these confessional expositions of the second commandment above is that they forbid *all images of God*, whether they were intended for worship, education, or artistic expression. This needs to be pointed out in light of those who say that images are forbidden only if they are used for worship.[72] To say that the second commandment and its interpretation/application are within this sphere of public or private worship only is to miss the point. Not only were the first four commandments given to God's people in the area of worship, the commandments were meant to be the comprehensive summary of the life of God's people. Those who say that images are forbidden, but only for worship, imply that we can fulfill the command of God by not having images in worship, while we have them in books or at home on our walls. The logical conclusion is that we can have idols, but just not in worship; we can take the Lord's name in vain all week, but not on Sunday. To say that the second commandment was written for the context of worship only, and therefore we can make pictures of Christ, the incarnate God, outside of worship, is like saying we can dishonor, murder, commit adultery, steal, lie, and lust after that which belongs to our unbelieving neighbors because we are only forbidden to do these things amidst the covenant community. This illegitimate division of the second commandment into purposes of worship and purposes of art/education was refuted by John Calvin in 1563, when he said,

> Some expound the words, "Thou shalt not make to thyself a graven image, which thou mayest adore;" as if it were allowable to make a visible image of God, provided it be not adored; but the expositions which will follow will easily refute their error. Meanwhile, I do not deny that these things are to be taken connectedly, since superstitious worship is hardly ever separated from the preceding error; for as soon as any one has permitted himself to devise an image of God, he immediately falls into false worship.[73]

Therefore, it is because of the biblical prohibition on images, because the incarnation meant that Jesus had real definable bodily features, because of the nature Christian eschatological hope, and because of the unified voice of the Reformed confessions and catechisms, that we as Reformed churches have a thoughtful, conscientious objection to portraying Jesus Christ for public worship and private devotional exercises as well as in art and movies, whether for expression, education, or as an evangelistic tool. This is what the Reformed churches have believed for five hundred years. This is the result of delving deeply into the Word of God and letting its commands and prohibitions affect our theology, life, and worship in our contemporary setting. Our position is not meant to suppress artistic expression or stunt the spiritual growth of God's people, but is meant to take God's commandment seriously, while also allowing his means, not ours, to dictate how we relate to him and learn from him in this age between his two advents.

2 God's Media: *Preaching*

O foolish Galatians! Who has bewitched you? It was before your eyes that Jesus Christ was publicly portrayed as crucified.

—St. Paul, Galatians 3:1

But may not pictures be tolerated in churches as books for the laity? No; for we should not be wiser than God, who will not have his people taught by dumb idols, but by the lively preaching of his Word.

—Heidelberg Catechism, Q&A 98[1]

"IT'S A CHANNEL for speeding up God's Word to get it into their hearts." So Jeffrey MacDonald recounted a "Reformed" pastor's advocacy of using video images as opposed to merely using words as a means of instruction. Statements like this show just how captive evangelical Christians have become to the idolatries of our culture. The philosophy of the day says we must treat people as consumers and give them what they want, when they want it. As the fast food chain Burger King says, "Have it your way." This philosophy in the culture has sadly become a philosophy of ministry.

One can well imagine this mind-set among the Israelites, who said in effect, "Moses, just hurry up and give us water; give us bread; give us quail." (Ex. 15:22–17:7) Providentially, the Lord taught them patience—for forty years! In doing so, he also teaches us the same lesson:

> Now these things took place as examples for us, that we might not desire evil as they did. . . . Now these things happened to them as an example, but they were written down for our instruction, on whom the end of the ages has come (1 Cor. 10:6, 11).

We can well imagine the desperate people in Jesus' time saying, "Hurry up and heal my daughter!" "Where were you when Lazarus was sick?" We can be thankful that Jesus did not "speed up" God's Word or else Lazarus and his family would not have come to know that Jesus was "the resurrection and the life" (John 11:25). They had to wait. They had to endure. They had to question.

We have seen man's medium for worshipping, evangelizing, and educating through images of God and Jesus Christ, which the Lord denounces in no uncertain terms in his Word and which the historic Reformed confessions reject as well. With all this negative discussion about why we ought not to have images, we may be left wondering whether God has left us without any means at all by which we can know and experience our Lord in living color.

God's Twofold Media

Having discussed images of Christ negatively, we proceed in the next two chapters with a positive presentation of the means that God *has* given us in the twofold means of the preached Word and visible sacraments. As early as 1543, John Calvin pointed out this twofold means in his *Inventory of Relics*, in which he satirically cataloged the relics of Christ and the saints of the Roman Church in contrast to the true means by which his people come to know him:

> But the first abuse, and, as it were, beginning of the evil, was, that when Christ ought to have been sought in his Word, sacraments, and spiritual influences, the world, after its wont, clung to his garments, vests, and swaddling clothes; and thus overlooking the principal matter, followed its accessory.[2]

As we saw in the previous chapter, this twofold means of Word and Sacrament by which we relate to God experientially was expressed in the Second Helvetic Confession. In it Heinrich Bullinger rejected the religious images of non-Christians as well as "Christian" religious images when he said:

> But that men might be instructed in religion, and put in mind of heavenly things and of their own salvation, the Lord commanded *to preach the Gospel* (Mark xvi.15)—not to paint and instruct the laity by pictures; *he also instituted sacraments*, but he nowhere appointed images (emphasis added).[3]

One final example of this emphasis on God's twofold media will suffice. In 1604 the English Puritan, John Dod (1549–1645), said in his exposition of the second commandment, "Therefore it is absurd to make an image of Christ . . . *look upon him in the Word and sacraments*" (emphasis added).[4]

In this chapter, then, we want to speak about the first of these two means, by discussing how the preaching of the Word of God, especially the preaching of the holy gospel, is the chief means whereby we come to worship God, evangelize the lost, and instruct children and adults in the Christian faith.[5] In this chapter we will focus on several New Testament texts, as well as the confessional teaching, which explain the nature and medium of preaching.

Preaching in the History of God's People

The centrality of preaching is seen throughout the history of the church, from its inception to its current form. The LORD God himself was the first preacher to his people in the Garden. After Adam's sin the LORD God announced the first gospel promise, saying, "I will put enmity between you and the woman, and between your offspring and her offspring; he shall bruise your head, and you shall bruise his heel" (Gen. 3:15). The Belgic Confession explains this proclamation of the LORD God, saying,

> We believe that our most gracious God, in his admirable wisdom and goodness, seeing that man had thus thrown himself into temporal and spiritual death, and made himself wholly miserable, was pleased to seek and comfort him when he trembling fled from his presence, promising him that He would give his Son, who should *be made of a woman, to bruise the head of the serpent,* and would make him happy.[6]

While Adam and Eve hid amidst the trees of the Garden, it was "our most gracious God" who sought and comforted Adam. How did he comfort Adam? God did so through preaching the gospel: "promising him that He would give his Son." After the LORD God's sermon he raised up a series of ancient preachers. Jesus called Abel a prophet (Luke 11:49–51), Jude said Enoch prophesied the coming of the Lord (Jude 14), and Peter called Noah a "herald of righteousness" (*dikaiosunes keruka*; 2 Peter 2:5). The point is that preaching has been a divinely exemplified and instituted medium from the beginning and came into its high point in the ministry of our Lord, his apostles, and in new covenant ministers.

As we delve into the meaning of preaching, and how it is God's substitute for our contrived media, it is important to remember that in the history of the church, as the ministry of the Word decreased, the medium of images increased. This was what St. Augustine wrote sixteen hundred years ago. Against those who wrote false gospels in the names of Peter and Paul, after seeing Roman art in which Peter and Paul were depicted as being with Christ, Augustine said, "Thus to fall most completely into error was the due desert of men who sought for Christ and His apostles not in the holy writings, but on painted walls."[7] Over one thousand years later the Puritan John Owen (1616–83) spoke even more forcefully, when he said,

> This, therefore, is evident, that the introduction of this abomination, in principle and practice destructive unto the souls of men, took its rise from the loss of an experience of the representation of Christ in the gospel, and the transforming power in the minds of men which it is accompanied with, in them that believe.[8]

Images were introduced, according to Owen, because the people of God lost their experience with Christ in the preaching of the gospel. Christ is experienced through preaching even as

Peter said to our Lord: “Lord, to whom shall we go? You have the words of eternal life” (John 6:68). It is to that preaching that we now turn in the pages of the New Testament.

John 6

In John 6 we read the account of Jesus’ bread of life discourse, in which he preached in living color the significance of who he was. Taking a meager five loaves and two fish and giving thanks for them, he gave them to his disciples and fed a multitude of five thousand. These took “as much as they wanted” (6:11) and ate “their fill” (6:12 cf. 26).

When he was found the next day on the other side of the lake, Jesus gave them his message. Some would see this as Jesus’ paradigm church growth seminar, as he used the felt needs of his hearers and dramatized who he was visually. Instead, this was Jesus’ church shrinkage seminar, as he called those who would follow him to understand who he was. He did nothing to “speed up God’s Word,” but called them to lifelong discipleship, meditation, and contemplation of the significance of his words. In a day like ours in which the professing church of Jesus Christ treats image bearers of God as demographics, seeking to get people in the door by satisfying their felt needs, we need the attitude of his faithful remnant of eleven disciples: “Lord, to whom shall we go? You have the *words* of eternal life” (6:68).

Jesus' preaching drove the tourists away but drew the seekers unto him.[9] Because of what Jesus said, almost all of his so-called disciples left him after saying among themselves, "This is a hard saying, who can listen to it?" (6:60) This Greek word for "hard" (*sklēros*) is used only one other time in the entire New Testament, in Jude 15, where Jude says that when Christ returns he will judge all unbelievers who say "harsh, unpleasant" things against him. Yet in John 6 it was Jesus who spoke the harsh words! When the tourists came to him, seeking more bread, Jesus announced that he was the bread of life (6:35); he was the food that endured for eternal life (6:27); the bread who gave life to the world (6:33); the bread who would satisfy their hunger (6:35). In order to eat this bread, one had to believe in Jesus, whom the Father sent (6:29). Unfortunately, they did not believe in him (6:36). Only those the Father gave him would come to him in faith (6:37). The crowds were fixated on his statement that he came down from heaven because they knew him as Joseph's son (6:41–42). They argued about his words instead of believing what the words signified. This is why Jesus said, "No one can come to me unless the Father who sent me draws him" (6:44). The one who was drawn would not eat manna as their fathers ate, who eventually died, but the heavenly bread, which was his flesh, and which would give eternal life (6:49–51). To this, they grumbled again, as the wilderness generation had done with Moses so many millennia ago. They could not understand that he would say they must eat his flesh (6:52). Therefore Jesus pressed his hard language, telling them that they had no life in themselves, but had to eat and drink Christ to have life (6:53–58).

Jesus' words were harsh because they cut down his disciples to size as hard-hearted, grumbling sinners like their fathers. His words magnified the grace of God and stripped his disciples of their pride and vanity. Jesus challenged his hearers, saying, "Do you take offense at this?" (6:61) This word "offense" (*scandalizei*) is the same word Paul uses in 1 Corinthians 1:23, where he says that the preaching of Christ crucified is a "scandal" and a "stumbling-block" to the Jews. He also says in Galatians 5:11 that we preach and believe the "scandal of the cross." The gospel is contrary to the natural man. It is outside of us. His words offended because they tell unbelievers that only one man has ever lived a perfect, righteous, and holy life and that they are dead and cannot do anything to save themselves. Jesus unambiguously puts to rest the notion that God helps those who help themselves.

Jesus' preaching caused his true disciples to stay with him. He asked them, "Do you want to go away as well?" (6:67) Jesus just went from having over five thousand followers to twelve—really eleven since Judas was an unbeliever. Jesus would not be called a success in the eyes of the mega-church pastors of our day, yet he is "our chief Prophet and Teacher" (Heidelberg Catechism, Q&A 31) and "chief Shepherd" of the church (1 Peter 5:4). This is why Simon Peter responded, saying, "Lord, to whom shall we go? You have the words of eternal life" (6:68). On the one hand false disciples left because of his harsh teachings, but true followers of the Lord find in those difficult, hard, unpleasant sayings the very words of eternal life. As Jesus said to them, "The words that I have spoken to you are spirit and life" (6:63).

What Jesus' temporary disciples called "hard" words were in fact the "words of eternal life" and "spirit and life." While Jesus' miraculous multiplication of bread and fish gave his followers temporary life, it was Christ, as proclaimed through the voice in living color, that gave spiritual and eternal life. Preaching must point to Christ, then, who is like bread, meat, and satisfying water; preaching must do as Jesus did, grabbing the attention of the hearers by speaking very vividly and metaphorically of Christ.

Romans 10

As was said in the introduction, the question we as Reformed Protestants ask in relation to movies about Jesus and their use as evangelism is this: "What *has* God promised to use as the means of communicating his saving grace?" It is not that we want to box God in, or truncate his message, but that God himself has ordained that he will work his mighty grace through mundane means. The means by which God creates faith in the hearts of sinners is the *preaching* of the gospel—nothing more and nothing less. We see this clearly taught in Romans 10.

In this chapter, Paul addresses the issue of the salvation of his fellow countrymen, the Jews. His "heart's desire and prayer" was that "they may be saved" (10:1). Unfortunately, their zeal for God was without knowledge (10:2) as they sought to make themselves righteous and would not "submit to God's righteousness" in Jesus Christ (10:3), who is "the end of the law for righteousness to everyone who believes" (10:4).

This righteousness was not one in which we bring Christ down or bring him up by our own efforts, but a righteousness that Moses spoke of, saying, "The word is near you, in your mouth and in your heart (that is, the word of faith that we proclaim)" (10:8). This word of gospel was for all, "For 'everyone who calls on the name of the Lord will be saved'" (10:13). In response, this was where Paul asked several important questions in relation to preaching:

> How are they to call on him in whom they have not believed? And how are they to believe in him of whom they have never heard? And how are they to hear without someone preaching? And how are they to preach unless they are sent? (10:14–15).

His conclusion was that "faith comes from hearing, and hearing through the word of Christ" (10:17). This *word* was the official, public speech that a sent preacher brings to the world on behalf of the Lord. Furthermore, what is so revealing is how Paul conceives of preaching. It is not information about Christ, but it is the means whereby Christ speaks. Look again at verse 14, which most translations translate to say, "And how are they to believe in him *of whom* they have never heard?" This translation would cause us to think that it is the preaching about Christ that brings one to faith. While it is true that preaching must relate the content *of whom* Jesus is, more importantly, the grammar of Paul's words teach us that preaching is Christ's voice. The New American Standard Bible and older American Standard Version translate the phrase rightly, "And how are they to believe in him *whom* [*hou*] they have never heard?" This is further confirmed by the end of verse 17, which says faith comes by the preaching of the word *of Christ* [*hrēmatos Christou*]. Christ is the subject of this word, not the object; meaning, he is the one speaking, not the one being spoken of.

Not only does Paul teach us here that Christ speaks through preaching, but that there is a clear connection between "hearing" the gospel preached and faith. Paul very well could have traveled with a troupe of actors to portray the life, death, and resurrection of Jesus. In fact, the Graeco-Roman culture was known for its great cultural expressions in plays written by some of the greatest playwrights and poets the world has ever seen. Yet the Christian God chose to use the foolish and weak means of preaching. However, in his article, Jeffrey MacDonald recounts one Reformed pastor as saying,

> We believe the Reformers missed something big. . . .
> When we limit the gospel message to the written and
> spoken text, we short-circuit it. We truncate it. . . .
> The soul is moved by more things than the word.

Yet is this how Paul speaks in Romans 10? After all, if "moving the soul" is our goal, there are more potent ways than having people passively look at a picture, or catatonically watch a movie clip they have probably seen many times already. What could move us more than hearing the very voice of Christ himself, accommodated through the ordinary voice of the week-by-week preaching ministry of the ordinary minister of the Word?

This is why as Reformed Protestants who confess the teaching of the Reformed catechisms and confessions, we reject art *as a medium to communicate the gospel,* whether for evangelism, or education, because preaching is *the primary* means God has ordained to save his people, enthrall their imaginations, and teach them. After all, preaching is not merely the voice of the minister, but the voice of Christ through the voice of the minister to grant faith in order to embrace Christ by faith alone.

1 Corinthians 1–2

One of the most instructive texts on preaching in the New Testament is 1 Corinthians 1:18–2:16. Here Paul contrasts the Greeks' desire for wisdom and the Jews' desire for signs with the foolishness of preaching Christ, God's wisdom signified upon the cross. What Paul says is that we do not preach mere wisdom, nor did God merely send a cosmic sign to be gazed upon, but that through preaching, the wisdom of God in sending his Son to be crucified saves his people. Paul begins by saying, "For the *word of the cross* is folly to those who are perishing, but to us who are being saved it is the power of God" (1:18). Preaching is through words, but those words are about the cross, the greatest visual sign there is of the justice and love of God. The ministers' words are not to be empty words, then, but words filled with significance and visual metaphor. Because the word of preaching is foolishness, both to the Greeks who could not conceive of a spiritual god becoming human like us in every way and to the Jews who could not conceive of the Messiah becoming a curse on the cross, Paul quotes from the prophet Isaiah, who denounced man's wisdom (1:19 cf. Isa. 29:14). In God's plan, what the world thought was foolish in its wisdom was really the wisdom of God (1:20–23, 25) and what the world thought was weak was really the power of God (1:24–25). The purpose of this method and message was to "shame the wise" and to "bring to nothing things that are" (1:27, 28) in order to bring glory and honor to himself through the *method* of preaching and the *message* of the preaching the cross of Christ (1:29–31).

Further, the *messenger* was foolish. This is why Paul continued in chapter 2 to say that when he came to the Corinthians it was not by "proclaiming to you the testimony of God with lofty speech or wisdom" (2:1), instead, it was by knowing "nothing among you except Jesus Christ and him crucified" (2:2). This meant he desired to experience the sufferings of Christ among them in hardship and persecution, just as Christ, just as them, being with them "in weakness and in fear and much trembling" (2:3). In his *Institutes of the Christian Religion*, John Calvin spoke of why God chose men to be the messengers of preaching, and not angels, saying,

> But as he did not entrust the ancient folk to angels but raised up teachers from the earth truly to perform the angelic office, so also today it is his will to teach us through human means. As he was of old not content with the law alone, but added priests as interpreters from whose lips the people might ask its true meaning, so today he not only desires us to be attentive to its reading, but also appoints instructors to help us by their effort. This is doubly useful. On the one hand, he proves our obedience by a very good test when we hear his ministers speaking just as if he himself spoke. On the other, he also provides for our weakness in that he prefers to address us in human fashion through interpreters in order to draw us to himself, rather than to thunder at us and drive us away. . . . For, among the many excellent gifts with which God has adorned the human race, it is a singular privilege that he deigns to

> consecrate to himself the mouths and tongues of men in order that his voice may resound in them. . . . the church is built up solely by outward preaching.[10]

God has chosen men to be his messengers, according to Calvin, for two beneficial reasons: first, it tests our obedience of whether we will hear God through men, and, second, it provides for our weakness, since we would be too timid to draw near to a thundering God.

Paul also spoke in 1 Corinthians 2 that the messenger's "weakness" came out in the outward *manner* of his preaching: "My speech and my message were not in plausible words of wisdom, but in demonstration of the Spirit and of power" (2:4). As with his words in chapter 1, all of this was "that your faith might not rest in the wisdom of men but in the power of God" (2:5). The great English Puritan William Perkins (1558–1602) explained the manner of preaching in lowly words, which was the way the Spirit demonstrated his power, when he said,

> To preach in the demonstration of God's Spirit is to preach with such plainness, and yet with such power, that even the least intellectually gifted recognize that it is not man but God himself who is teaching them. Yet at the same time, the conscience of the mightiest may feel not man but God reproving them through the power of the Spirit.[11]

It seems obvious, then, that the images of Christ so popular in the movies these days for the purposes of evangelism and education have a method, messenger, manner, and even message that is contradictory to the preaching of the gospel. One says the gospel is limited by words (and thus, the Word is insufficient) while the other says the *gospel is a word*:

"For the *word* of the cross is folly to those who are perishing, but to us who are being saved *it is the power of God*" (1 Cor. 1:18). Are we not moved by *God's power* through preaching?

"For since, in the wisdom of God, the world did not know God through wisdom, it pleased God *through the folly of what we preach* to save those who believe" (1 Cor. 1:21). Are we wiser than God, who has ordained preaching?

"For Jews demand *signs* and Greeks seek wisdom, but we *preach* Christ crucified" (1 Cor. 1:22–23). Are we more interesting than God who would have his grace communicated through words?

"For the *foolishness of God* is wiser than men, and *the weakness of God* is stronger than men" (1 Cor. 1:25). Are we more effective than God with our humanly devised images, art, and movies?

Galatians 3

Besides Paul's words on sacred rhetoric in 1 Corinthians, some of his most astonishing words on preaching were to the

Galatian Christians: "O foolish Galatians! Who has bewitched you? It was before your eyes that Jesus Christ was publicly portrayed as crucified" (Gal. 3:1). These words are astonishing because the Greek word for "publicly portrayed" speaks about holding up a sign for all to see. What Paul is saying is that we as preachers, if we dare call ourselves this, are to hold up publicly Jesus Christ crucified on a banner in such a way that our hearers can "see" him dying before us on a cross. The astonishing thing is that we are to do this *through preaching the word of the cross!*

This text has stirred the greatest exegetes and preachers in the history of the church to elaborate upon it. In the ancient church, John Chrysostom (347–407), arguably the greatest preacher of that period, explained this verse in his homily to his parish, saying,

> Yet he was not crucified in Galatia, but at Jerusalem. His reason for saying, "among you," is to declare the power of faith to see events which are at a distance. He says not, "crucified," but, "openly set forth as crucified," signifying that by the eye of faith they saw more distinctly than some who were present as spectators.[12]

The Galatians were able to see Jesus Christ upon the cross through faith because he was as clearly displayed to them in words, as if a banner were held up in their midst. In his lectures through Galatians, the German reformer Martin Luther (1483–1546), said the following:

> Christ was so lively described before them, that they might handle Him with their hands. . . . I have with great pains and diligence set forth Christ plainly before your eyes, yet doth this profit not at all. . . . there is no painter with his colours can so lively set out Christ unto you, as I have painted Him by my preaching: and yet ye remain most miserably bewitched. What did I paint then? Even Christ Himself.[13]

Luther invokes the metaphor, speaking of his preaching as painting Christ before his people. This preaching of Christ ought to be so vivid and understandable that our hearers might be able to touch Christ with their hands, so to speak.

John Calvin also spoke eloquently on Galatians 3:1 in the various places he touched upon this verse: in his *Institutes*, his commentary, and his sermon. In his *Institutes*, he said,

> What purpose did it serve for so many crosses—of wood, stone, silver, and gold—to be erected here and there in churches, if this fact had been duly and faithfully taught: that Christ dies on the cross to bear our curse [Gal. 3:13], to expiate our sins by the sacrifice of his body [Heb. 10:10], to wash them by his blood [Rev. 1:5], in short, to reconcile us to God the Father [Rom. 5:10]? From this one fact they could have learned more than from a thousand crosses of wood or stone. For perhaps the covetous fix their minds and eyes more

> tenaciously upon gold and silver than upon any word of God.[14]

Foreshadowing the words of Heidelberg Catechism, Q&A 98, Calvin spoke of clearly and simply teaching God's people through words rather than by relics and tangible images. In his commentary upon Paul's words in Galatians 3:1, Calvin spoke eloquently and prophetically in the following way of the preaching of the cross:

> Such, he tells them, was the clearness of his doctrine, that it was not naked doctrine, but the express, living image of Christ. They had known Christ in such a manner, that they might be almost said to have seen him. . . . To shew how energetic his preaching was, Paul first compares it to a picture, which exhibited to them, in a lively manner, the image of Christ. But, not satisfied with this comparison, he adds, 'Christ hath been crucified among you,' intimating that the actual sight of Christ's death could not have affected them more powerfully than his own preaching. . . . The meaning therefore is, that Paul's doctrine had instructed them concerning Christ in such a manner as if he had been exhibited to them in a picture, nay, 'crucified among them.' Such a representation could not have been made by any eloquence, or by 'enticing words of man's wisdom,' (1 Cor 2:4) had it not been accompanied by

> that power of the Spirit, of which Paul has treated largely in both the Epistles to the Corinthians. Let those who would discharge aright the ministry of the gospel learn, not merely to speak and declaim, but to penetrate into the consciences of men, to make them see Christ crucified, and feel the shedding of his blood. When the Church has painters such as these, she no longer needs the dead images of wood and stone, she no longer requires pictures; both of which, unquestionably, were first admitted to Christian temples when the pastors had become dumb and been converted into mere idols, or when they uttered a few words from the pulpit in such a cold and careless manner, that the power and efficacy of the ministry were utterly extinguished.[15]

Preachers need to learn from Calvin's words here, and parishioners need to expect from their preachers what Calvin says. Preaching must be clear and as it were the living images of Christ, not "naked doctrine." The preaching ministry is not a lecture on theological points, but the means by which Christ speaks to his people through the living voice of a minister. May it be said of our ministry, that our people "might be almost said to have seen him." This liveliness of preaching is shown in that Paul compares it to a picture, but one that is alive to the point that "the actual sight of Christ's death could not have affected them more powerfully than his own preaching."

Calvin's application of this passage to ministers was that we would "penetrate into the consciences of men, to make them see Christ crucified, and feel the shedding of his blood."

Finally, in his sermon upon this text, Galatians 3:1–3, Calvin proclaimed to his congregation in sixteenth century Geneva the necessity of the Word over images, which proclamation is instructive for us:

> Moreover we warned also, which are the true pictures or paintings to lead us to God. The Papists say we must have remembrances to teach us, and that images are the books of the unlearned which are not apt to conceive higher doctrine: but hath Saint Paul spoken here but to three or four folk? No. It is generally, and to all Christians without exception, as well as to great and small, that he saith that when the gospel is preached, then Jesus Christ is painted out lively, and we must look upon him, not with the fleshly eyes of our bodies, but with the spiritual eyes of faith. Then seeing it is so, let us learn that we have no need of images and puppets to teach us what is necessary for our salvation, neither need we a piece of wood, stone or other such pelting stuff, to put us in remembrance of God, (for in all those things there is nothing but vanity and falsehood) but we have need to have God's word preached, and to endeavor and travail to make the same familiar with us, that we may there behold God in his lively image, that is

> to say in the person of our Lord Jesus Christ his only son.[16]

Roughly one hundred years later in the same city of Geneva, the theologian, Francis Turretin, expounded upon Galatians 3:1. In his exposition he said,

> When the apostle says that "Jesus Christ had been evidently set forth before the eyes of the Galatians, crucified among them (Gal. 3:1), he does not speak of fashioning of images of the crucifix (which were made either by the brush of the painter or the chisel of the sculptor), but of the preaching of the Gospel, by which he is exhibited to us as crucified. . . . [T]he honor of the image does not pass over to the prototype and exemplar, unless he himself (which is the exemplar) has so willed or ordained. But if on the contrary *he has prohibited any image of himself to be made or to be honored*, he is treated injuriously if anyone goes against his will."[17]

What Galatians 3:1 says, and what the quoted expositors taught, was that although portraying Christ in pictures, paintings, statues, and movies is forbidden, the Spirit creates faith within us through the read and preached Word as it interacts with the human intellect, imagination, and psyche. The gospels are marvelously crafted stories. This is why Dorothy Sayers called the story of Scripture "the greatest drama ever told." As with any story we tell, there is an amount of commonality with the story as written, and the reader as experienced. The writers intentionally wrote this way to evoke in us wonder, reverence, and a vivid view of Jesus' person and work. Although the Galatians, and we, were not outside Jerusalem to see Jesus crucified, when we hear the Word proclaimed, the we understand what a man looks like, what it feels like to experience physical and emotional pain, and what a cross looks like. The Spirit uses these common aspects of our understanding not to create a mental picture of Jesus hanging upon a cross, but to give us a sense of what was happening.

As a way of grasping this, we can use a helpful distinction. Although his theology was hardly orthodox, Rudolph Bultmann made a great distinction between the *existentielle* and the *existential*. The first is my personal involvement in the story, while the latter is my being a spectator or an abstract questioner of the story. Although we do not know what Jesus looked like or looks like now, when we read of our dear Savior picking up little children, we cannot help being personally affected and involved in that as we think of being held as a child, or holding a child. The stories are not merely meant to convey *existential* truth about the tenderness of Jesus and the nature of entering the kingdom in that story, but also my *existentielle* involvement by recalling in my mind what it looks like and feels like for a child to be held by someone who loves her. We may not know the details of the story, who was there, or what Jesus was wearing, but we can imagine a first century Jewish rabbi, standing in a crowd, picking up a little child who has been playing in the dirt all day.

The application of Galatians 3:1 is obvious in the context of this book. Many assume that *The Passion* and other visual means are somehow a form or method of preaching the gospel. As we have said, as those who believe wholeheartedly in the absolute sovereignty of God in the salvation of humans, we believe that God is able to use movies like this precisely because he is totally free and sovereign. As the Psalmist says, "Our God is in the heavens; he does all that he pleases" (Ps. 115:3). Nevertheless, the ends do not justify the means. Simply because God is able to do something does not mean that he will do something, or even that he must do something we expect.

Our confidence must be that God definitely uses the preached gospel to seek, save, and sanctify the lost. He has promised to do so. On the contrary, it is mere speculation for us to say that God is going to use a movie for outreach purposes when he has not revealed that he will do so in his Word. Movies, books, so-called "ministries" that churches have invented, such as a "clowns for Jesus ministry," and even the witnessing of the ordinary Christian do not have the same promises attached to them as preaching. This may be a shock, but our forefathers' teaching was clear: the lively preaching of the gospel of our Lord Jesus Christ is the ordained means of God to save.

In terms of the church's ministry of witness and evangelism, while we do not need to agree that *The Passion* was "the greatest evangelistic opportunity in 2000 years," we certainly must encourage, support, and labor to witness in our neighborhoods and preach the gospel from the pulpit week by week.

Heidelberg Catechism

Question and Answer 65

Moving from these key New Testament texts on preaching we come to the Protestant Reformers' teaching on preaching in their catechisms and confessions. The place to begin is the Heidelberg Catechism and question and answer 65, which asks, "Since, then, we are made partakers of Christ and all his benefits by faith only, whence comes this faith?" This question summarizes all that has gone before in the section on grace, namely, that the heart of who we are as Reformed churches is that we are justified by grace alone, through faith alone, in Christ alone. The question moves us from our belief that faith alone in Jesus Christ alone is the sole instrument of our justification and union with Christ to the question of what is the instrument of that very faith. The answer is, "The Holy Ghost works it in our hearts *by the preaching of the holy Gospel*, and confirms it by the use of the holy Sacraments" (emphasis added).[18]

In this question and answer, the Catechism follows the words of Paul, already quoted, when he says, "So faith comes from hearing, and hearing through the word of Christ" (Rom. 10:17). What we are taught is that faith is "worked" in us by the Holy Spirit who uses the preaching of the gospel as the means by which we are given the faith to be justified. The Catechism links the Word and the Holy Spirit, which was a common theme in the Reformers' theology.[19] The Heidelberg Catechism particularly applies this to the inseparability of the Spirit and the *preached* Word to create justifying faith within us, in particular the preaching of the gospel.[20] The Catechism describes the preaching of the gospel as the chief means of grace (*media gratiae*) whereby the Holy Spirit causes sinners to become saints.[21]

There is a vital link between the work of the Spirit and preaching. Nowhere in Scripture are we promised this link between the Spirit and images. Because the Word and Spirit are so linked together, the Word can be said to be the external form of the Spirit, and the Spirit the internal power of the Word.[22] Caspar Olevianus (1536–87), one of the authors of the Heidelberg Catechism, called the minister of the gospel the "organ of the Holy Spirit" (*Spiritus Sancti organum*),[23] and, the preaching of the gospel the "chief testimony and principle organ of the Holy Spirit by which the substance of the covenant is offered to us."[24] In his exposition of question 20, which introduces question 21 and the nature of true faith, Olevianus said, "In sum, Christ is offered to us by the Father in no other way than through the foolishness of preaching, or the promise of the gospel (1 Cor. 2)."[25]

Question and Answer 67

The primary purpose of the preaching of the gospel, as said above, is the creation of faith in the hearts of sinners. The Catechism also specifies the content of the preaching that the Holy Spirit uses to create faith. It is not the preaching of the law that the Holy Spirit uses to create faith, but the preaching of the gospel—the preaching of Christ. Zacharius Ursinus noted this vital distinction when he said, "The instrumental cause of faith in general is the word of God. . . . The chief and peculiar instrument of justifying faith is the preaching of the gospel."[26] It is not the preaching of the Bible in general, nor is it the law, which only reveals to us our guilt and gratitude (Q&A 3), but it is the proclamation of Christ—the gospel—that brings lifeless sinners to life. We learn this in question and answer 67:

> Are both these, then, the Word and the Sacraments, designed to direct our faith to the sacrifice of Jesus Christ on the cross as the only ground of our salvation?
>
> Yes, truly; for the Holy Ghost teaches in the Gospel, and by the holy Sacraments assures us, that our whole salvation stands in the one sacrifice of Christ made for us on the cross.[27]

According to question 67, preaching is to point people to "Christ crucified" (1 Cor. 1:23). While it is generally true that this preaching should have as its hearers all men, in this question we learn that the preaching of the gospel pertains to those who already believe. Preaching is "designed to direct *our faith*" (emphasis mine) to Christ.

We also notice in relation to this answer that the Holy Spirit teaches his people through the preaching of the holy gospel. This is what Jesus spoke of when he said the Holy Spirit was to be sent to "teach you all things and bring to your remembrance all that I have said to you" (John 14:26). We are taught about Christ by Christ himself through his Spirit in the voice of ministers.

We learn a very important truth as ministers in these questions: Christians need to hear the gospel, too. Christ-centered, evangelistic preaching is not just for the world of unbelievers, but also for the covenant community. This is so vital for us. The world is bombarded by false Christianity today, which teaches that "evangelism" is what we do on special occasions at rallies, revivals, or crusades. Even more disturbing is the trend among non-denominational churches today to turn the church into a smorgasbord to satisfy felt-needs, or the redefinition of the gospel to mean Christians in social action. Professing Christians and the world are being duped every week. We need to be aware of this trend among our parishioners and in our own ministries, as the temptation to get greater numbers affects us all. Let us, though, be different from the world, but also from the host of worldly churches, and preach the gospel; for although it is foolishness and seemingly weak, it is the power of God to salvation.

Questions and Answers 83–84

Preaching is also described in the Heidelberg Catechism in connection with the kingdom of God. Here we notice the conjunction and harmonious activity of both the Word as it is preached and Spirit, working in concert to bring about the powerful work of God the Son, who is the head of the church (Col. 1:18). What is it about the Word preached, that when it is accompanied by the Spirit's power, it is able to gather from the mass of sinful humanity a chosen communion? The answer is found in relation to question and answer 83 and 84 and our belief concerning the keys of the kingdom, in general, and the key of preaching, specifically. Besides church discipline, "The preaching of the Holy Gospel" is the other key of Christ's kingdom, "By which two things the kingdom of heaven is opened to believers and shut against unbelievers" (Q&A 83).[28] So then, "How is the kingdom of heaven opened and closed by the preaching of the holy Gospel?"

> In this way: that according to the command of Christ, it is proclaimed and openly witnessed to believers, one and all, that as often as they accept with true faith the promise of the Gospel, all their sins are really forgiven them of God for the sake of Christ's

> merits; and on the contrary, to all unbelievers and hypocrites, that the wrath of God and eternal condemnation abide on them, so long as they are not converted; according to which witness of the Gospel, will be the judgment of God both in this life and in that which is to come.[29]

Through the voice of men, amazingly, the very gates of heaven itself are opened and closed to those who hear. Surely this gets at the heart of what the Catechism teaches us about preaching! Preaching is that solemn and earnest proclamation of the way of escape from the wrath of God in hell by means of the life, death, and resurrection of Jesus Christ the Lord. If we would just believe that, our preaching would be transformed, our people emboldened and empowered to be salt and light, our worship given a sense of holy transcendence, and the world brought to their knees with us.

Question and Answer 98

As we have already referenced, the Heidelberg Catechism speaks of the "lively preaching" of the Word in question and answer 98, in contrasting to educating the church with images of God and Jesus Christ. This "lively" preaching is to be what we discussed above in relation to Galatians 3:1—that preachers are to preach Christ in such a way that it is as if the congregation can even see him dying before them on a cross.

Since preaching is the chief means of grace, whereby Christ himself speaks to create faith in us and to open the doors of his heavenly kingdom, it is not to be a theological lecture, which puts people to sleep. It is also not to be an ear-tickling sermonette for Christianettes or moralistic brow-beating. Instead, preaching is to be a passionate and bold pronouncement of what God has done in Christ. In explaining the second commandment, the Catechism contrasts two methods of teaching God's people in worship. The people of God are not to be taught by "dumb idols" [i.e., mute idols], but instead "by the lively preaching of his Word."[30]

To say that preaching is "lively" is to say that it passionately and clearly shows forth Jesus Christ and all his benefits. We see a striking text to this effect in the New Testament when the apostle Paul rebuked the Christians in Galatia. In that epistle he said, "It was before your eyes that Jesus Christ was publicly portrayed (*proegraphē*) as crucified" (Gal. 3:1). We see the full force of this Greek word brought out by multiple translations of this verb: *clearly portrayed* (NIV, NKJV), *openly set forth* (ASV), *openly and graphically set forth and portrayed* (AMP), and *as clearly as though I had shown you a signboard with a picture of Christ dying on the cross* (NLT). True preaching of Christ is lively because the "real presence" of the Holy Spirit is found in the voice of the minister, as well as the elements of the sacraments. This is why the *Second Helvetic Confession* summarized the Reformed view of preaching when it said, "Wherefore when this Word of God is now preached in the church by preachers lawfully called, we believe that the very Word of God is preached, and received of the faithful" (I.4).[31]

To preach the Word in a lively manner is to have Paul's passion, but more importantly, it is to preach Christ so clearly, so plainly, that it is as if we ourselves were holding up a large placard with a picture of Christ on the cross before our people. Our preaching must be vivid, clear, earnest, and plain. This is a part of what Paul was saying in 1 Corinthians 2:4: "And my speech and my message were not in plausible words of wisdom, but in demonstration of the Spirit and of power." The prince of preachers, Charles Haddon Spurgeon (1834–92), spoke of this plain yet vivid style of preaching, when he said,

> We must throw all our strength of judgment, memory, imagination, and eloquence into the delivery of the gospel; and not give to the preaching of the cross our random thoughts while wayside topics engross our deeper meditations.[32]

Question and Answer 103

Finally, the context in which the preaching of the law and the gospel is to occur is expressed in the Heidelberg's exposition of the fourth commandment, in question and answer 103. God's will for the Christian in relation to the Sabbath Commandment, is, in part, "That I, especially on the day of rest, diligently attend church, to learn the Word of God . . ."[33]

In Heidelberg, as in all the Reformed churches, this diligent attendance at church to "learn the Word of God" occurred twice on the Lord's Day. In the morning, the Scriptures were proclaimed chapter by chapter, book by book, according to what is called the *lectio continua* method, while in the afternoon, the Scriptures were proclaimed via their summary in the Heidelberg Catechism. These catechetical sermons have a long history in the Christian church as exemplified in the ancient church order, the *Didache*,[34] and the catechetical sermons of such great ancient preachers as Cyril of Jerusalem,[35] John Chrysostom,[36] Theodore of Mopsuestia,[37] and Augustine.[38]

The practice of Heidelberg in holding a second service on the Lord's Day in which public catechesis was conducted was a feature of all Reformed churches.[39] In the Netherlands, the practice of catechetical preaching goes back to at least 1566, when the Latin edition of the Catechism was divided into 52 Lord's Days and the Dutch Reformed pastor Petrus Dathenus added the Catechism to his *Psalter*. This practice was first made binding on Reformed ministers at the 1586 Synod of the Hague and reiterated in the Church Order of the Synod of Dort (1618–19). Article 68 of the Dort Church Order said,

> The Ministers everywhere shall briefly explain on Sunday, ordinarily in the afternoon sermon, the sum of Christian doctrine comprehended in the Catechism which at present is accepted in the Netherland Churches, so that it may be completed every year in accordance with the division of the Catechism itself made for that purpose.[40]

This is still the practice of Reformed churches whose heritage is in the Netherlands, such as the United Reformed Churches in North America, the Canadian Reformed Churches, the Protestant Reformed Churches, the Free Reformed Churches, the Netherlands Reformed Churches, and the Heritage Reformed Congregations. In fact, the venerable Presbyterian, B. B. Warfield, once said of the Christian Reformed Church, "Two things keep the small Christian Reformed Church straight in the midst of a crooked ecclesiastical world, its Catechism preaching and its catechetical instruction of its youth."[41]

The Synod of Dort gave much guidance for catechetical preaching as there were many complaints about it. Among the reasons catechetical preaching was not done were ministers failing to hold afternoon services, the peoples' negligence in going to work or play instead, ministers who served two or more parishes, the Remonstant party's opposition, and the government's failure to uphold the Sabbath day. The advice of the Synod was five-fold:[42]

1. The decision of the Synod of 1586 mandating catechism preaching was reiterated. As well, the catechism was to be explained "in brief sermons, and in such a way that the children also could understand it."[43]

2. Second services were to be held despite low attendance. In fact, catechism services were to be held "even though the minister had to preach to his family alone."[44]

3. The government was asked to uphold the Sabbath day.
4. As much as possible, churches should have their own minister.
5. Church visitors were to take close note of whether a minister was preaching catechism sermons; if not, he was to be reported to Classis for censure.

The seriousness of the Synod in relation to catechetical preaching was a result of its principles, as expressed in the Heidelberg Catechism, among other places. In this sixteenth-century catechism, we learn that preaching is the central point of Reformed worship because it is the primary way God meets with his people to create faith in the Christ who justifies, open the gates of his eternal kingdom, and sanctify them throughout their life in preparation for the life to come. This is why we take so much time every Lord's Day to say, "Thus saith the Lord."

The Canons of Dort

One last place to look for our understanding of why preaching is the primary means of education and evangelism is the Canons of Dort.[45] The great Synod of Dort was held from November 13, 1618 to May 9, 1619 in the armory of the Dutch city of Dort to deal with the disturbance in the Dutch Reformed churches by the followers of the deceased professor of theology at the University of Leiden, Jacobus Arminius. This national synod of the Dutch churches was turned into an international synod at the urging of King James I of England and others. Invitations were sent throughout Europe to Reformed countries and churches to send their best theologians to help settle this turmoil in the Reformed churches, which was bound to spread throughout Europe.[46] These delegates wrote up a statement of faith and rejection of errors called "canons" (*kanōn*, "rule"), dealing with the issues of election, Christ's atonement, human depravity, the grace of the Holy Spirit, and the perseverance of the saints.

The Relationship Between Preaching and Election

Canon I.1 begins with three basic biblical truths, that: 1) all men have sinned in Adam (Rom. 5:12), 2) all men lie under the curse (Gal. 3:10, 13; cf. Isa. 24:5–6), and 3) all men are deserving of eternal death (Ps. 51:1–5, 53:1–3; Rom. 3:9–20, 5:12, 18–19). Despite our sin, the immeasurable love of God was made known to those in this situation, as Canons I.2 says:

> But "in this the love of God was manifested, that he sent his only-begotten Son into the world," "that whoever believes in him should not perish but have everlasting life" (1 John iv.9; John iii.16).[47]

Canon I.3 goes on to speak of how sinners come to know this love of God in Christ:

> And that men may be brought to believe, God mercifully sends the messengers of these most joyful tidings to whom he will, and at what time he pleaseth; by whose ministry men are called to repentance and faith in Christ crucified. "How then shall they call on him in whom they have not believed? And how shall they believe in him of whom they have not heard? And how shall they hear without a preacher? And how shall they preach, except they are sent?" (Rom. 10:14–15).[48]

God the Father draws us to Jesus Christ so that we might receive his love by "mercifully send[ing] the messengers of these most joyful tidings." It is "by [their] ministry [that] men are called to repentance and faith in Christ crucified." God ordains the *ends* and the *means* of salvation.

Later in I.7 the Canons define the doctrine of election as God's unchangeable and eternal good pleasure in choosing a certain number out of the sinful situation mentioned before. This article continues to say that "this elect number . . . God hath decreed to give to Christ to be saved by him, and effectually to call and draw them to his communion *by his Word and Spirit*" (emphasis added).[49]

Former Calvin Theological Seminary professor, Anthony Hoekema (1919–88), described this feature of the Canons of Dort, in which God elects sinners from eternity, but then sends Christ, the Holy Spirit, and preachers to bring them to salvation, as the *Missio Dei*, the mission of God. In an article on the Canons of Dort, he said that this document "teaches the indispensability of missions."[50] He went on to say,

> We could therefore say that the main focus of the Canons is on the *Missio Dei* (the mission of God): God's redemption of the cosmos through the saving work of Jesus Christ applied to the hearts of his people by the Holy Spirit.[51]

There is an intimate link between God's predetermination of the end—our salvation—and his determination to use preaching as the means to attain that end. Believing in election is not exclusive of evangelism and preaching. In fact, what election teaches us is that God's eternal plan takes form in ordinary men, who use ordinary language, and who speak to ordinary people.

The Relationship Between Preaching & the Spirit's Application of Redemption

The largest discussion of preaching in the Canons occurs in the third and fourth heads of doctrine, entitled, "Of the Corruption of Man, his Conversion to God, and the Manner thereof."[52] Why is it necessary to preach the gospel to bring the elect to faith in Jesus Christ?

> What, therefore, neither the light of nature nor the law could do, that God performs by the operation of his Holy Spirit

> through the word or ministry of reconciliation: which is the glad tidings concerning the Messiah, by means whereof it hath pleased God to save such as believe (III/IV.6).[53]

The reason preaching is necessary is that the law, both natural and revealed, cannot save us; only God can save us, and he has determined to use the ministry of men to bring about that salvation. This head of doctrine continues to describe what preaching does, when it teaches that through preaching "God . . . seriously promises eternal life and rest to as many as shall come to him, and believe on him" (III/IV.8) and that Christ is "offered" to men (III/IV.9).[54] This promise and offer of Christ himself in preaching, though, is not simply pronounced, only to leave sinners to decide. Instead, the Canons teach that in those in whom God does his work of regeneration, the gospel is not merely "*externally* preached to them," but that God himself "powerfully illuminates their minds by his Holy Spirit." This "efficacy of the . . . regenerating Spirit" actually opens the closed heart, softens the hardened heart, circumcises the uncircumcised, infuses new qualities into the will, quickens from being dead (III/IV.11).[55] Again, Canon III/IV.12 reiterates the important point that the regeneration of the sinner is

> . . . nowise effected merely by the *external* preaching of the gospel, by moral suasion, or such a mode of operation that, after God has performed his part, it still

> remains in the power of man to be regenerated or not, to be converted or to continue unconverted.[56]

On the contrary, it is by means of preaching that the Holy Spirit does a "supernatural work . . . not inferior in efficacy to creation or the resurrection from the dead."[57] This third and fourth head of doctrine is concluded with a summary article that teaches the supernatural work of God in regenerating lifeless sinners and that this work is accomplished by the use of the means of preaching:

> As the almighty operation of God, whereby he prolongs and supports this our natural life, *does not exclude, but requires the use of means*, by which God of his infinite mercy and goodness hath chosen to exert his influence; so also the before-mentioned supernatural operation of God, by which we are regenerated, *in nowise excludes or subverts the use of the gospel*, which the most wise God has ordained to be the seed of regeneration and food of the soul. Wherefore as the Apostles, and the teachers who succeeded them, piously instructed the people concerning this grace of God, to his glory and to the abasement of all pride, and in the mean time, however, neglected not to keep them by the sacred precepts of the gospel, in the exercise of the Word, the sacraments and discipline; so, even to this day, be it far from either instructors or instructed to presume to tempt God by

> separating what he of his good pleasure hath most intimately joined together (III/IV.17).[58]

The first clause in this article speaks of God's use of means to give us earthly life. It is then ended with a semicolon, signifying another thought after the first thought. The second clause, then, continues this theme of the use of means, but this time with our heavenly life. As we need the means of food to live earthly lives, so too we need the means of food to live heavenly lives: bread for our bodies, the Word for our souls. Further, this canon ends with an application to us: just as the apostles instructed their people and kept them nourished by the Word, sacraments, and discipline, so too we must do the same with the means God has appointed.

The Relationship Between Preaching and the Perseverance

This final thought above leads us into the fifth head of doctrine, "Of the Perseverance of the Saints." Here we are taught that not only do we still have a sin nature, inherited from Adam's fall, but that we are still prone to fall into serious sins. It is in these times of stumbling spiritually, that God preserves us. The Canons teach us how God preserves us, saying,

> For in the first place, in these falls he preserves in them the incorruptible seed of regeneration from perishing or being totally lost; and again, *by his Word and Spirit, he certainly and effectually renews them to repentance*, to a sincere and godly sorrow for their sins, that they may

> seek and obtain remission in the blood of the Mediator, may again experience the favor of a reconciled God, through faith adore his mercies, and henceforward more diligently work out their own salvation with fear and trembling (V.7).[59]

Not only does our almighty God choose to use the means of his Word to effect a new creation in us, but he also chooses to use the means of his Word to renew us when we fall from the new estate into which we have been placed. This use of the means of the Word to renew is later picked up in terms of our preservation in grace. In Canon V.14, we read:

> And as it hath pleased God, by the preaching of the gospel, to begin this work of grace in us, so he preserves, continues, and perfects it by the hearing and reading of his Word, by meditation thereon, and by the exhortations, threatenings, and promises thereof, as well as by the use of the Sacraments.[60]

Here we read of the beginning of our new life (regeneration), the continuation of our new life (sanctification), but also the perfection of our new life (glorification), all of which are effected by means of the preaching of the of the holy gospel.

Finally, the Canons speak about the doctrine of assurance and the source of our knowledge of assurance. Head V.10 speaks of our assurance as coming from "a serious and holy desire to preserve a good conscience, and to perform good works" as well as "the testimony of the Holy Spirit, witnessing with our spirit, that we are children and heirs of God."

Most importantly, though,

> This assurance, however, is not produced by any peculiar revelation contrary to, or independent of the Word of God but springs from faith in God's promises, which he has most abundantly revealed in his Word for our comfort.[61]

Conclusion

To summarize all this material, then, we have seen that, contrary to the spirit of the age that desires to use images to communicate and convey information, the Scriptures teach us that the primary means whereby God communicates is the preaching of the Word of God. This preaching is a means of grace, as it is used by the Holy Spirit to regenerate us, to give us faith to embrace Jesus Christ for our justification, and to sanctify and preserve us in the grace of God. As such, preaching is not merely about Christ, but it is the voice of Christ, despite the lowly means and manner. In this, though, the Spirit demonstrates the power of God, for his glory, our comfort, and the humbling of human pride.

3 God's Media: *Sacraments*

The cup of blessing that we bless, is it not a participation in the blood of Christ? The bread that we break, is it not a participation in the body of Christ? Because there is one bread, we who are many are one body, for we all partake of the one bread.

—St. Paul, 1 Corinthians 10:16–17

We believe that our gracious God, on account of our weakness and infirmities, hath ordained the Sacraments for us, thereby to seal unto us his promises, and to be pledges of the good will and grace of God towards us, and also to nourish and strengthen our faith, which he hath joined to the word of the gospel, the better to present to our senses, both that which he signifies to us by his Word, and that which he works inwardly in our hearts. . . . For they are visible signs and seals of an inward and invisible thing, by means whereof God worketh in us by the power of the Holy Ghost. . . . For Jesus Christ is the true object presented by them, without whom they would be of no moment.

—Belgic Confession of Faith (1561), article 33[1]

IN 754, the Synod of Constantinople condemned the creation of images of Jesus Christ. This Synod occurred in the midst of great controversy in the Christian church over images of Christ between the *iconophiles* (icon-lovers)/*iconodoules* (icon-servers) and the *iconoclasts* (icon-smashers). This iconoclastic council rejected images, summarizing its position:

> Whoever, then, makes an image of Christ, either depicts the Godhead which cannot be depicted, and mingles it with the manhood (like the Monophysites), or he represents the body of Christ as not made divine and separate and as a person apart, like the Nestorians.[2]

Images of the divine nature of Christ cannot be made, as we have seen already (Ex. 20:4 cf. John 1:18; 1 Tim. 6:16), because this means the image is of a mixture of his divine and human natures. Images of the human nature cannot be made because this means the image is merely of his human nature and therefore separates his two natures.[3] In light of that condemnation, this ancient Synod went on to say the following:

> The only admissible figure of the humanity of Christ, however, is bread and wine in the holy Supper. This and no other form, this and no other type, has he chosen to represent his Incarnation.[4]

The connection this Synod in late antiquity made between man-made images of Christ and Christ's ordained image of himself in Holy Communion is one that David VanDrunen reflected upon in his previously mentioned article. In that article he said: "The relationship of images of Christ with the Eucharist especially is an issue worth much more exploration."[5] Whereas the preached Word is audible, the sacraments are visible images before us of God's own appointment. John Calvin also alluded to this connection between images and the Supper in his *Institutes*, where he spoke in contrast to the superstitious rites of the churches, saying,

> It seems to me unworthy of their [the churches] holiness for them to take on images other than those living and symbolical ones which the Lord has consecrated by his Word. I mean Baptism and the Lord's Supper, together with other rites by which our eyes must be too intensely gripped and too sharply affected to seek other images forged by human ingenuity.[6]

The purpose of this chapter is to explore the visible and tangible pictures of Christ in the Lord's Supper, as well as holy baptism, which are the two sacraments of the new covenant church of Jesus Christ. These are God's ordained media for his church, to see, touch, smell, and taste the grace of his Son, Jesus Christ. As we saw in the previous chapter, God has ordained the medium of preaching as the chief and primary means by which he makes and molds the faith of his people. To this audible Word he has also given visible Words that picture, image, and signify Christ to us. These do not come from our own desires, as man's media, but are God's media to reach down to us. Instead of man's media, which we have seen seek to reach upward to God, God's media of Word and Sacrament reached downward from the Lord to us. Our images are law, as we seek to create an experience with God by our own efforts, but because the sacraments are gospel, they are God's effort to enter into a relationship with us. In a word, images are rooted in man's imagination; the sacraments are rooted in God's institution.

Baptism

Jesus left his disciples with no pictures or descriptions of himself, but he has left us with baptism, the dramatic sign of entry into the community of faith by virtue of being washed with water. For those who believe, the significance of the waters of baptism are that here we arise a new creation as the earth arose out of the waters (Gen. 1) and as Noah and his household were saved through the Flood (Gen. 6–9); here we leave the kingdom of this world and enter the kingdom of Christ as Israel crossed the sea on dry land (Ex. 14); here we pass as Israel from the death of the wilderness into the life of the Promised Land (Josh. 3); here we undergo a death and resurrection as we are identified with Christ (Rom. 6); and here we are washed by the Spirit himself (Titus 3).

We might be tempted to think that we are somehow limiting God by our rejection of images and placing a high premium on words in preaching. We may even be tempted to think that he desires our wise and creative ways to reach an image-saturated culture. What is more dramatic than baptism, though? Even more, it is not an image merely to be seen passively, but a tangible element to be experienced and touched.

Beginning with Baptism

In his *Large Catechism*, Martin Luther spoke of the Christian life in these words: "A Christian life is then nothing else than an ongoing daily Baptism, once begun and always continuing."[7] He also described baptism as the greatest jewel with which to adorn our bodies and souls, as well as our daily garment to be worn.[8]

One may very well question the validity of such an approach to the Christian life, placing baptism at the forefront. Instead, our debt to Evangelicalism leads us to want to think in terms of the Christian's conversion, faith, etc., as the beginning of the Christian life. Yet, using baptism as an organizing image and event, we have something to grasp, something tangible to relate our lives to. After all, try as hard as you may to remember the moment you were converted, can you ever be sure? Instead, we see the font before the people of God every Lord's Day and its waters used on many occasions. The liturgy for *Public Profession of Faith: Form Number 1*, which many Reformed churches use today, conceives of the Christian life in this way, when it asks, "Second: Do you openly accept God's covenant promise, which has been signified and sealed unto you in your baptism."[9] Being received into the church has its reference point in holy baptism and our embrace of its significance for our lives.

The New Testament

Baptism is the visual and vivid picture of the Christian life. All throughout the New Testament, the authors refer or allude to baptism time and again in their reminders, exhortations, and teaching. When Jesus sent out his apostles in Matthew 28:18–20, in the so-called "Great Commission," he charged them to make disciples. It is instructive that disciple-making is described in this order: baptizing and teaching. When Paul wanted to speak powerfully and vividly of the Christian's entrance into a new kind of life, leaving behind sin and entering righteousness, he pointed to baptism (Rom. 6). When Paul spoke about lawsuits among believers and the sinful actions in the congregation at Corinth, he point them to baptism: "But you were washed" (1 Cor. 6:11). He used baptism as an illustration of our unity with Israel and each other (1 Cor. 10, 12). When he spoke of our being children of Abraham, he spoke about baptism (Gal. 3). When he wanted to proclaim that we are complete in Christ and do not need to undergo circumcision, he referred to baptism (Col. 2). To convey what it means to be regenerated he alluded to baptism (Titus 3). This is not peculiar to Paul, as the writer to the Hebrews used baptism as a call to worship (Heb. 10), James as a way of teaching that God's name was placed upon us (James 2), and Peter that we are like Noah, saved through a flood (1 Peter 3).

Re-Birth

As a sacrament, baptism is one of the "visible signs and seals of an inward and invisible thing" (Belgic Confession, art. 33).[10] This means that, along with Holy Communion, baptism is the gospel-made-visible. The visibility of baptism speaks of birth, or, re-birth, to be exact. It is as if we go into the womb and come out with new life. The historic baptismal liturgy of the Reformed churches opens by saying,

> . . . we with our children are conceived and born in sin,
> and therefore are children of wrath, so that we cannot
> enter the kingdom of God, except we be born again.
> This, the dipping in or sprinkling with water
> teaches us.[11]

Here the *Form* draws upon Psalm 51:5 and Ephesians 2:3, which say that we were "brought forth in iniquity," conceived "in sin" by our mothers, and are "by nature children of wrath." These texts teach us "that we cannot enter the kingdom of God." The only way is by being "born again," as Jesus taught in John 3. Further, the liturgy explains the meaning of baptism in the name of the Triune God, saying in part,

> . . . when we are baptized into the Name of the Father, God the Father witnesses and seals unto us that He makes an eternal covenant of grace with us and adopts us for His children and heirs.[12]

Initiation

Baptism is also the sacrament of *initiation*. The Belgic Confession says by baptism "we are received into the Church of God, and separated from all other people and strange religions, that we may wholly belong to him whose ensign and banner we bear" (art. 34).[13] Our confession follows John Calvin here, who said, "Baptism is the sign of the initiation by which we are received into the society of the church, in order that, engrafted into Christ, we may be reckoned among God's children.[14] Later, the Genevan theologian Francis Turretin spoke of this initiation aspect of baptism, saying,

> For it is evident that two things are specially necessary that life should be given to us; then that (when given) it should be conserved and supported: the nativity is adumbrated by baptism; the nutrition by the Supper. Hence the former is called 'the sacrament of initiation' and the laver of regeneration; the latter 'the sacrament of confirmation and of nutrition.' By baptism, we are regenerated; by the Supper we are nourished unto eternal life; by that we are received into the covenant, and by this we are kept in.[15]

This initiatory aspect of baptism finds its parallel in the Old Testament rite of circumcision. In the place of circumcision, Jesus "has instituted the sacrament of baptism" for the New Covenant. What this teaches us is that both circumcision and baptism's place is that of an initiatory sign of membership in the covenant. There is one covenant of grace and this covenant always has a sign, yet, the administration of the one covenant of grace is multi-faceted. Under the old administration, circumcision was the rite of initiation, while under the New, baptism is the sign of initiation. As the confession says, the sign initiates one "into the Church of God," that is, into the visible, covenant community. As an initiatory rite, baptism separates us "from all other people and strange religions" as the sign "that we may wholly belong to Him whose mark and ensign we bear." Under the old administration of the covenant, slaves bought with money as well as foreigners who desired to joined Israel were marked out with the sign and shown to belong to the LORD (Gen. 17:12–13; Ex. 12:43–48). We, too, have been marked out in baptism, in which "the honorable name" was placed upon our foreheads (James 2:7; Rev. 22:4).[16]

This initiation was what Jesus spoke of in Matthew 28, when he charged his apostles with making disciples, "baptizing them . . . teaching them" (Matt. 28:19, 20). Further, after Peter preached his sermon on Pentecost, and those who were "cut to the heart" asked, "Brothers, what shall we do," Peter responded,

"Repent and be baptized" (Acts 2:37, 38). Notice, then, Luke's editorial statement after this: "So those who received his word were baptized, and there were added that day about three thousand souls" (Acts 2:41).

The Life of Baptism

Baptism also speaks of *life and death.* The baptism *Form* says, "And when we are baptized into the Name of the Son, the Son seals unto us that He washes us in His blood from all our sins, incorporating us into the fellowship of His death and resurrection." Later, we pray that God will look upon the one baptized "and incorporate them by Thy Holy Spirit into Thy Son Jesus Christ, that they may be buried with Him through baptism into death and be raised with Him in newness of life."

Although baptism is administered once, its benefits do not end when the water is poured, Christ's words uttered, and prayer is made. As the Belgic Confession says, "Neither does this Baptism only avail us at the time when the water is poured upon us and received by us, but also through the whole course of our life."[17] Baptism is the sacrament of initiation into lifelong discipleship. Discipleship involves repentance from sin ("buried with Him through baptism into death") and faith in the Lord Jesus Christ ("raised with Him in newness of life"). We ought to recall our baptism continually as a testimony that we belong to the Lord, and therefore, that we ought to live to his glory. As Calvin said, "This we must believe: we are baptized into the mortification of our flesh, which begins with our baptism and which we pursue day by day and which will, moreover, be accomplished when we pass from this life to the Lord."[18]

This life of the baptized is vividly described in the prayer before baptism as "nothing but a constant death." Thus, baptism teaches us to "humble ourselves before God, and seek for our purification and salvation apart from ourselves." It also calls us "unto new obedience, namely, that we cleave to this one God, Father, Son, and Holy Spirit; that we trust Him, and love Him with all our heart, with all our soul, with all our mind, and with all our strength; that we forsake the world, crucify our old nature, and walk in a godly life."

We pray for this, asking the Lord "that they [those being baptized], daily following Him [Christ], may joyfully bear their cross, cleaving unto Him in true faith, firm hope and ardent love" and that they might "manfully fight against and overcome sin, the devil, and his whole dominion."

One practical way this lifelong benefit of baptism is used is when the Christian struggles with sin and doubt. As John Calvin said, "Therefore, as often as we fall away, we ought to recall the memory of our baptism and fortify our mind with it, that we may always be sure and confident of the forgiveness of sins."[19] Baptism is a reference point for the Christian. It is like a compass that points us due north, to Christ and our life in him. This is what Martin Luther is reported to have said to himself every morning: *baptizatus sum*, "I am baptized," and when he was asked, "How do you know you are a Christian," he said, "I am baptized." This is a statement of faith for the one who embraces Christ and his benefits signified in baptism.

Our Reformed forefathers thought in these terms as well. In late 1538 and early 1539, Martin Bucer helped organize the Reformed church in the region of Hesse, which was led by the great Prince Philipp. In the *Church Order of Cassel*, Bucer wrote the liturgy for the Hessian church. In the "Order for Confirmation and the Laying on of Hands," a child that had been baptized and catechized came before the church to profess his faith and be received at the Lord's Table. The opening questions and answers are:

> Q. Are you a Christian?
> A. Yes.
>
> Q. How do you know?
> A. Because I have been baptized in the name of the Father, Son, and Holy Spirit.[20]

Then the minister and child recite questions about the Apostles' Creed. After these questions, there are several on the meaning of the sacraments. These questions and answers begin by asking,

> Q. Are you in the Church and fellowship of Christ?
> A. Yes.

> Q. How did you enter?
> A. Through holy Baptism.[21]

Furthermore, the catechism used in Calvin's French-speaking congregation in Strasbourg, as found in the 1542 *Psalter*, asks a child, as he makes a profession of faith, the following questions:

> Q. Are you, my son, a Christian in fact as well as in name?
> A. Yes, my father.
>
> Q. How do you know yourself to be?
> A. Because I am baptized in the name of the Father and of the Son and of the Holy Spirit.[22]

Participating in Baptism

Baptism is a visual event in which we are called to participate all our life. No explanation of this is better than the Westminster Larger Catechism, question 167, which asks, "How is our baptism to be improved by us?"[23] The word "improve" comes from a late-Middle English word meaning, "to turn (something) into profit." The Larger Catechism, then, is asking us how we who have been baptized can benefit from it. After saying, "The needful but much neglected duty of improving our baptism, is to be performed by us all our life long, especially in the time of temptation, and when we are present at the administration of it to others," the catechism goes on to give several ways to benefit from baptism.

First, we participate and benefit from our baptism by understanding our baptism: "by serious and thankful consideration of the nature of it, and of the ends for which Christ instituted it, the privileges and benefits conferred and sealed thereby, and our solemn vow made therein."

Second, we participate and benefit from our baptism by being humbled by the reason for baptism: "by being humbled for our sinful defilement, our falling short of, and walking contrary to, the grace of baptism, and our engagements."

Third, we participate and benefit from our baptism by receiving the assurance it brings to us: "by growing up to assurance of pardon of sin."

Fourth, we participate and benefit from our baptism by engaging in its significance, the death and life of the sinner: "and of all other blessings sealed to us in that sacrament; by drawing strength from the death and resurrection of Christ, into whom we are baptized, for the mortifying of sin, and quickening of grace."

Fifth, we participate and benefit from our baptism by continually coming out of the water, as it were, to live by faith: "and by endeavoring to live by faith."

Sixth, we participate and benefit from our baptism by living holy lives in its remembrance: "to have our conversation in holiness and righteousness, as those that have therein given up their names to Christ."

Seventh, we participate and benefit from our baptism by learning to love those baptized in the same way as us: "and to walk in brotherly love, as being baptized by the same Spirit into one body."

This medium of baptism, then, draws us tangibly into the life that God has created for us, sent his Son to bring us, and that the Spirit unites us to by faith, unlike the medium of images, which can only touch us through the singular sense of the eyes.

Lord's Supper

As those who have dramatically crossed the sea, our Lord also continues to nourish us tangibly by the Lord's Supper, as we see, touch, smell, and taste his body and blood. Here we are lifted up in heavenly hope, when we shall partake with our Lord (Matt. 26) in the marriage Supper of the Lamb (Rev. 19). The dramatic aspect of the Lord's Supper (in contrast to movies of Christ) was vividly described by John Calvin, who said,

> Nevertheless, we do not deny that the sacrifice of Christ is so shown to us there [Lord's Supper] that the spectacle of the cross is almost set before our eyes—just as the apostle says that Christ was crucified before them (Gal. 3:1).[24]

It is this aspect of the holy Supper that we seek to understand here, so that we will come to know the Lord more fully as he reveals himself in the living colors of bread and wine.[25]

Controversial Yet Comforting

The Lord's Supper divided the Protestant churches from the Roman Catholic Church because of Rome's doctrine of *transubstantiation*. This doctrine teaches that the substance of bread and wine are transformed into Christ's flesh and blood. Later this doctrine was supplemented by the Council of Trent's decree in 1562 that the Eucharist was a propitiatory sacrifice, that is, it was meant to turn away the wrath of Almighty God.

This controversy also divided Protestants from Protestants. Early in the Reformation Martin Luther met with Ulrich Zwingli at the Marburg Colloquy in 1529 to unite Wittenberg and Zurich. They agreed on fourteen points of doctrine but disagreed on "whether the true body and blood of Christ are bodily present in the bread and wine."[26] Whereas Luther vehemently believed Christ's words to be literal, even writing the words, "This is my body," upon the table in front of him, Zwingli believed them to be symbolical only, and thus, the Lord's Supper was only a memorial of Christ's past work. These two opposing camps of Protestants were sought out for reconciliation over a period of decades by the mediating positions of Philip Melanchthon, Luther's successor, and Martin Bucer, the great Strasbourg pastor. Later Zwingli's successor, Heinrich Bullinger, moved closer to the center with a position described as parallelism, which meant that as surely as a communicant ate and drank bread and wine he also fed upon Christ. John Calvin brought the two camps closer with his view described as *instrumentalism*. This meant that not only did a communicant eat bread, on the one hand, and partake of Christ, on the other, *a la* parallelism, but also that the bread and wine were the means by which the Holy Spirit mysteriously communicated Christ to his people.

The Sacrament of Nutrition

While article 34 of our confession describes baptism as the one-time sacrament of *initiation*, article 35 describes the Lord's Supper as the ongoing sacrament of *nutrition*. We can see this in the biblical terms used for this sacrament, which communicate the biblical imagery of a covenant meal. It is called the *breaking of the bread* (Acts 2:42), the *Lord's Supper* (1 Cor. 11:20), the *Lord's Table* (1 Cor. 10:21), *communion* or *fellowship* (1 Cor. 10:16), which is what occurs around a table, and the *Eucharist* or *thanksgiving* (1 Cor. 10:16) because it is a festive meal. In the same way the Belgic Confession opens in article 35, saying,

> We believe and confess that our Savior Jesus Christ did ordain and institute the Sacrament of the Holy Supper, to nourish and support those whom he hath already regenerated and incorporated into his family, which is his Church.[27]

Following this is a lengthy paragraph explaining the language of nourishment for both our bodies and souls. The "regenerated" have a twofold life. One the one hand they have a corporal ("bodily") and temporal life described as the result of their "first birth" and which "is common to all men." This life is supported and nourished by God who uses the means of bread, that is to say, food. On the other hand the "regenerated" have a spiritual and heavenly life described as the result of their "second birth." This life was "effected by the word of the gospel, in the communion of the body of Christ," and therefore is not common to all, as earthly life is, but is "peculiar to God's elect."

As is earthly life, the heavenly life is also supported and nourished by God, who sent the bread from heaven, our Lord Jesus Christ (John 6). He "nourishes and strengthens the spiritual life of believers, when they eat him, that is to say, when they apply and receive him by faith in the Spirit."[28] What is so important in these words is that in contrast to Zwingli, both Reformed and Lutheran Protestants taught the necessity of sacraments for our faith. This is what the confession goes on to say in these words: "Christ . . . hath instituted an earthly and visible bread as a Sacrament of his body, and wine as a Sacrament of his blood" to represent to us himself, the true food and drink of our souls. The purpose of this sacrament is that,

> As certainly as we receive and hold this Sacrament in our hands, and eat and drink the same with our mouths . . . we also do as certainly receive by faith (which is the hand and mouth of our soul) the true body and blood of Christ our only Savior in our souls, for the support of our spiritual life.

Manner of Partaking

The confession states that we receive Christ in the Lord's Supper. We notice the way the Supper is explained that the key to navigating through the "Supper strife" of the Reformation is the relevance of the Holy Spirit and faith, which is the gift of the Spirit.

We can speak of the bread as the body and the wine as the blood of Christ because the signs and thing signified are united by the incomprehensible work of the Holy Spirit. To use a human analogy, think about a wedding. At a certain part of the ceremony the man and woman both say, "With this ring, I thee wed." Yet the ring itself does not make marriage, but because the sign (ring) and thing signified (unending love), are so united we use this language in our ceremonies. This is precisely what God does in Scripture when he speaks of the rainbow (Gen. 9), circumcision (Gen. 15), and the cup as his covenant (1 Cor. 11).

This is the background to the confession's language about not eating the body and drinking the blood of Christ by the mouth (*manducatio oralis*). We do not eat the bread and wine in the same manner as we eat the body and blood. One mouth eats the outward signs, while the other, faith, eats the inner thing signified:

> Now, as it is certain and beyond all doubt that Jesus Christ hath not enjoined to us the use of his sacraments in vain, so he works in us all that he represents to us by

> these holy signs, though the manner surpasses our understanding and cannot be comprehended by us, as the operations of the Holy Ghost are hidden and incomprehensible. In the mean time we err not when we say that what is eaten and drunk by us is the proper and natural body and the proper blood of Christ. But the manner of our partaking of the same is not by the mouth, but by the Spirit through faith. Thus, then, though Christ always sits at the right hand of his Father in the heavens, yet doth he not, therefore, cease to make us partakers of himself by faith. This feast is a spiritual table, at which Christ communicates himself with all his benefits to us, and gives us there to enjoy both himself and the merits of his sufferings and death, nourishing, strengthening, and comforting our poor comfortless souls by the eating of his flesh, quickening and refreshing them by the drinking of his blood.[29]

Our Reformed fathers saw this understanding of the Supper as a return to the theology of the ancient church. After all, the Reformation was about re-forming the church, not re-storing it. And so we as Protestants are the true catholics. The greatest evidence of the teaching that Christ is fed upon by faith through the work of the Holy Spirit is from the ancient Eucharistic liturgy, in which the minister calls out to the congregation, "Lift up your hearts," and the people respond, "We lift them up to the Lord!"

It is by lifting up our heart to heaven and by being elevated by the Spirit that we feed upon Christ's true and natural body and blood by faith, the mouth of our souls (cf. John 6:35, 51, 56). Another example is in the words of Athanasius, the great defender of orthodox doctrine:

> For how many bodies of him would be sufficient for eating, that there might be food for the whole world? But on this account he made mention of his ascension into heaven that he might draw them away from a corporal understanding and they might understand that the flesh of which he had spoken was the heavenly food and the spiritual nourishment to be given by him from above.[30]

What lies behind such an idea, in the teaching of the Reformed, is the doctrines of the person and work of Christ. After he came to earth in the incarnation, lived a perfect life, "was crucified, dead, and buried," our Lord rose again and then ascended back into heaven. The confession mentions this when it says "though Christ always sits at the right hand of His Father in the heavens." Furthermore, the reason such a statement about his work in the ascension is so relevant to the Lord's Supper is what we believe about the person of Christ. He is one person with two natures. Reformed theologians have always been mindful of confessing the catholic creeds, especially the Athanasian Creed and Definition of Chalcedon, which so mysteriously confess this ineffable doctrine: "it is necessary to everlasting salvation that [we] also believe rightly the Incarnation of our Lord Jesus Christ" (§29). In the Athanasian Creed we confess as catholic Christians that our Lord is God and man (§30)—"God of the substance of the Father, begotten before the worlds; and man of the substance of His mother, born in the world" (§31). Furthermore, he is "equal to the Father as touching His Godhead, and inferior to the Father as touching His manhood (§33). Finally, he is "One altogether, not by confusion of substance, but by unity of person" (§36).

Liturgical Setting

The Reformed churches rejected the practice of private Masses and therefore confessed a strong doctrine of the corporate nature of the Lord's Supper, following the language of Paul, who says that the church "came together" to partake of the Supper (1 Cor. 11:17–22). The confession follows suit, saying,

> Lastly, we receive this holy Sacrament in the assembly of the people of God, with humility and reverence, keeping up among us a holy remembrance of the death of Christ our Saviour, with thanksgiving, making there confession of our faith and of the Christian religion. . . . In a word, we are excited by the use of this holy Sacrament to a fervent love towards God and our neighbor.[31]

This paragraph also refers to the participants in the Lord's Supper. Those who have "rightly examined" themselves are invited to come to this spiritual feast. This "right examination" is described in terms of humility, reverence, remembrance, thanksgiving, and confession of the Christian religion.

Participating in Communion

As with baptism, it is important to say a word about our ongoing participation in Holy Communion. Again, the Westminster Larger Catechism gives us a helpful outline for participating in the sacrament of the Lord's Supper, asking in question 174, "What is required of them that receive the sacrament of the Lord's Supper in the time of the administration of it?"[32] The answer begins, "It is required of them that receive the sacrament of the Lord's Supper, that, during the time of the administration of it . . ." As with baptism, this answer goes on to list the practical way we can receive the most benefit from the Lord's Supper.

First, we participate by being attentive to the sacred ordinance that is in our midst: "with all holy reverence and attention they wait upon God in that ordinance."

Second, we participate by being observant of the ritual itself: "diligently observe the sacramental elements and actions."

Third, we participate by being discerning that it is the Lord's body and blood that we partake of: "heedfully discern the Lord's body."

Fourth, we participate by being affectionate towards our Lord: "and affectionately meditate on his death and sufferings, and thereby stir up themselves to a vigorous exercise of their graces."

Fifth, we participate by having an amount of self-judgment for our sins: "in judging themselves, and sorrowing for sin."

Sixth, we participate by being stirred up to a zealous spiritual appetite: "in earnest hungering and thirsting after Christ."

Seventh, we participate by feeding upon Christ spiritually: "feeding on him by faith, receiving of his fulness, trusting in his merits, rejoicing in his love, giving thanks for his grace."

Eighth, we participate in the knowledge of the fact that Holy Communion is a covenant renewal: "in renewing of their covenant with God, and love to all the saints."

Conclusion

The sacraments of baptism and the Lord's Supper, as we have seen, are the God-ordained means that Scripture reveals to us that God uses not only to incorporate us into the church in a dramatic way, but to nourish us mysteriously as members of the church. They enlist our participation with all our senses and faculties. We see the waters poured over a child or adult and the bread and wine before us; we hear the promises of God associated with these visible means; we touch the water and taste the bread and wine; we smell the wine. As image-bearers of God, we were made to receive the extraordinary and dramatic work of God in us by these ordinary means of his appointment. Although they may not seem to do the work the way we want it done, nevertheless they are the means whereby the Spirit works in us powerfully and subtly.

Conclusion

As we think about man-made images of Jesus Christ, our image-saturated culture, and what the Word of God teaches us about their prohibition, and as we consider his prescription of Word and sacraments, we are led to becoming a contented people. As pilgrims in the wilderness without an ultimate resting place in this life, we must not covet that which God has not given us nor what the world tells us that we need. Instead, as children of our heavenly Father, we are to be content with his means of creating faith in us and confirming us in faith. With the Psalmist we must ever pray and sing:

> O LORD, my heart is not lifted up;
> my eyes are not raised too high;
> I do not occupy myself with things
> too great and too marvelous for me.
> But I have calmed and quieted my soul,
> like a weaned child with its mother;
> like a weaned child is my soul within me
> (Ps. 131:1–2).

Our gracious God has given us his Word and two sacraments as the media by which he communicates to his image bearers. In this age between Christ's two comings, he has not left us with images of himself, and he has not authorized us to seek to depict artistically, portray evangelistically, or display worshipfully any image of himself, but instead we must see him by means of his divinely-ordained audible and visible, ordinary means.

If we desire beautiful art, we can look at creation, which God himself sculpted and painted for our enjoyment (Ps. 19) or we can use the imagination he has given us to depict and interpret his creation. If we desire a way to educate our children, what better way than by the preaching of the Word of God, in which the greatest story ever told is narrated to a living people, that is sung in the Psalms and hymns of the church, and that is expressed in the historic liturgy, creeds, and confessions of Christ's church. If we seek to be faithful to Christ's commission while also being relevant to an image-based society, we must trust God's promise to seek and to save by means of his Word, and to meet with us dramatically and experientially in the preaching event and in the celebration of the sacraments. These means were described by the writer of the epistle to the Hebrews in the context of apostasy, where he said,

> For it is impossible, in the case of those who have once been enlightened [baptism], who have tasted the heavenly gift [Lord's Supper], and have shared in the Holy Spirit, and have tasted the goodness of the word of

> God [preaching] and the powers of the age to come, and then have fallen away, to restore them again to repentance (Heb. 6:4–6).

If this sounds foolish, then you are right.

God has determined to work in foolish ways. Accordingly, no one can say our religion is about us, is about great crowds, or is about money. It is about Christ, who, though we have not seen him, will reveal himself in glory from heaven and take us to his side for eternity. Let us not attempt a sneak peek on canvas, in clay, on paper, or on the silver screen, but let us with great anticipation await the day when we will see him as he truly is, in living color.

Scripture Index

Confessions Index

Bibliography

a' Brakel, Wilhemus. *The Christian's Reasonable Service,* trans. Bartel Elshout, 4 vols. (Ligonier, PA: Soli Deo Gloria Publications, 1992).

An Introduction to the Heidelberg Catechism, ed. Lyle D. Bierma, Texts & Studies in Reformation & Post-Reformation Thought (Grand Rapids: Baker, 2005).

Athanasius. *The Letters of Saint Athanasius Concerning the Holy Spirit,* trans. C. R. B. Shapland (New York: The Philosophical Library, 1951).

Augustine. *A Harmony of the Gospels,* trans. S. D. F. Salmond, ed. M. B. Riddle, in *Nicene and Post-Nicene Fathers: First Series,* 14 vols. (1888; Peabody, Massachusetts: Hendrickson Publishers, Inc., reprinted 2004).

——. *City of God,* trans. Marcus Dods (New York; The Modern Library, 1993).

Barnes, Peter. *Seeing Jesus: The Case Against Pictures of Our Lord Jesus Christ* (Edinburgh: Banner of Truth Trust, 1990).

Bullinger, Heinrich. *The Decades of Henry Bullinger,* ed. Thomas Harding, 2 vols. (Grand Rapids: Reformation Heritage Books, 2004).

Baird, Charles W. *The Presbyterian Liturgies: Historical Sketches* (Eugene, Oregon: Wipf & Stock Publishers, 2006).

Baynard, Chuck. *Teaching Classic Reformed Theology in the 21st Century, Teacher's Manual: The Second Helvetic Confession* (n.d.). Found at http://www.christianobserver.org/Files/helvetic.pdf.

Boettner, Loraine. *Roman Catholicism* (Philadelphia: The Presbyterian and Reformed Publishing Company, 1962).

Calvin, John. "An Admonition, Showing the Advantage Which Christendom Might Derive From an Inventory of Relics," ed. and trans. Henry Beveridge, in *Selected Works of John Calvin, Tracts and Letters: Volume 1,* ed. Henry Beveridge and Jules Bonnet, 7 vols. (Grand Rapids: Baker, 1983).

——. "Catechism of the Church of Geneva," in *Selected Works of John Calvin: Tracts and Letters: Volume 1,* ed. Henry Beveridge and Jules Bonnet, 7 vols. (Grand Rapids: Baker, 1983).

——. *Commentaries on the Epistle to the Galatians,* trans. William Pringle, Calvin's Commentaries, 22 vols. (Grand Rapids: Baker, reprinted 1996).

——. *Commentaries on the First Book of Moses Called Genesis: Volume 1,* trans. John King, Calvin's Commentaries, 22 vols. (Grand Rapids: Baker, reprinted 1996).

——. *Commentaries on the Four Last Books of Moses Arranged in the Form of a Harmony: Volume Second,* trans. Charles William Bingham, Calvin's Commentaries 22 vols. (Grand Rapids: Baker, reprinted 1996).

——. *Commentaries on the Four Last Books of Moses Arranged in the Form of a Harmony: Volume Third,* trans. Charles William Bingham, Calvin's Commentaries 22 vols. (Grand Rapids: Baker, reprinted 1996).

——. *Institutes of the Christian Religion,* ed. John T. McNeill, trans. Ford Lewis Battles (Philadelphia: The Westminster Press, 1960).

——. *Sermons on Galatians* (Audubon, New Jersey: Old Paths Publications, 1995).

Clark, R. Scott. *Caspar Olevian and the Substance of the Covenant: The Double Benefit of Christ,* Rutherford Studies in Historical Theology (Edinburgh: Rutherford House, 2005).

Crisis in the Reformed Church, ed. Peter Y. De Jong (Grand Rapids: Reformed Fellowship, Inc., 2008).

Curtis, Edward M. "The Theological Basis for the Prohibition of Images in the Old Testament." *Journal of the Evangelical Theological Society* 28:3 (September 1985).

Dod, John. *A Plaine and Familiar Exposition of the Tenne Commandements,* (London, 1604).

Duke, Alastair. *Reformation and Revolt in the Low Countries* (London: Hambledon and London, 2003).

——. "The Netherlands," in *The Early Reformation in Europe,* ed. Andrew Pettegree (1992; Cambridge: Cambridge University Press, reprinted 1998).

Durham, James. *The Law Unsealed: or, A Practical Exposition of the Ten Commandments. With a Resolution of Several Momentous Questions and Cases of Conscience* (Edinburgh: D. Schaw, 1802).

Eire, Carlos M.N. *War Against the Idols: The Reformation of Worship from Erasmus to Calvin* (Cambridge: Cambridge University Press, 1986).

Erskine, Ralph. *Faith No Fancy: Or, a Treatise of Mental Images* (Philadelphia: William M'Culloch, 1805).

Frame, John. *The Doctrine of the Christian Life* (Phillipsburg: P&R, 2008).

Gregory the Great, *Register of the Epistles of Saint Gregory the Great,* trans. James Barmby, in *Nicene and Post-Nicene Fathers: Second Series,* ed. Philip Schaff and Henry Wace, 14 vols. (Peabody, Massachusetts: Hendrickson Publishers, Inc., reprinted 2004).

Grigg, Robert. "Aniconic Worship and the Apologetic Tradition: A Note on Canon 36 of the Council of Elvira." *Church History* 45.4 (December 1976): 428–33.

Heideman, Eugene P. "God the Holy Spirit," in *Guilt, Grace, and Gratitude: A Commentary on the Heidelberg Catechism,* ed.Donald J. Bruggink (New York: The Half Moon Press, 1963).

Hoekema, Anthony. "The Missionary Focus of the Canons of Dort," *Calvin Theological Journal* (November 1972).

Horton, Michael S. "How the Kingdom Comes." *Christianity Today* 50:1 (January 2006).

——. *Lord and Servant: A Covenant Christology* (Louisville: Westminster John Knox Press, 2005).

——. "Seekers or Tourists?: Or the Difference Between Pilgrimage and Vacation." *Modern Reformation* 10:4 (July/August 2001): 12–18.

——. *The Law of Perfect Freedom* (Chicago: Moody Press, 1993).

House, Paul R. "Examining the narrative of Old Testament Narrative: An Exploration in Biblical Theology." *Westminster Theological Journal* 67:2 (Fall 2005): 229–45.

Hyde, Daniel R. *God With Us: Knowing the Mystery of Who Jesus Is* (Grand Rapids: Reformation Heritage Books, 2007).

——. "Lift Up Your Hearts: Increasing the Use of the Sursum Corda." *Reformed Worship* 82 (December 2006): 33–35.

——. "The Holy Spirit in the Heidelberg Catechism." *Mid-America Journal of Theology* 17 (2006): 211–37.

——. "We Confess: Article 34." *The Outlook* 56:6 (June 2006): 10–14.

——. "We Confess: Article 35." *The Outlook* 56:7 (July/August 2006): 12–15.

——. *With Heart and Mouth: An Exposition of the Belgic Confession* (Grandville: Reformed Fellowship, 2008).

Irenaeus, *Against Heresies,* in *Ante-Nicene Fathers,* ed. Alexander Roberts and James Donaldson, 10 vols. (1885; Peabody, Massachusetts: Hendrickson Publishers, Inc., reprinted 2004).

Jerome, *Letter 51,* trans. W. H. Fremantle, G. Lewis, and W. G. Martley, in *Nicene and Post-Nicene Fathers: Second Series,* 14 vols. (1893; Peabody, Massachusetts: Hendrickson Publishers, Inc., reprinted 2004).

John Chrysostom, *Commentary on Galatians,* rev. Gross Alexander, in *Nicene and Post-Nicene Fathers: First Series,* ed. Philip Schaff, 14 vols. (1889; Peabody, Massachusetts: Hendrickson Publishers, Inc., reprinted 2004).

John Damascene, *On Holy Images* (London: Thomas Baker, 1898).

Julius Africanus, *Chronography,* in *Ante-Nicene Fathers,* ed. A. Cleveland Coxe, 10 vols. (1886; Peabody, Massachusetts: Hendrickson Publishers, Inc., reprinted 2004).

Kline, Meredith G. "Divine Kingship and Son of God in Genesis 6:1–4." *Westminster Theological Journal* 24 (1962): 187–204.

LaShell, John K. "Imagination and Idol: A Puritan Tension." *Westminster Theological Journal* 49:2 (1987): 305–34.

Luther, Martin. *Commentary on Galatians,* trans. Erasmus Middleton, ed. John Prince Fallowes (Grand Rapids: Kregel Classics,1979).

——. *Luther's Large Catechism: A Contemporary Translation with Study Questions,* trans. and ed. F.Samuel Janzow (Saint Louis: Concordia Publishing House, 1978).

MacDonald, G. Jeffrey. "Reformed Protestants No Longer See Images as Idolatrous." *Christianity Today* 48 (December [Web-only] 2004). Available at http://www.ctlibrary.com/ct/2004/decemberweb-only/12–6-12.0.html.

Marnef, Guido. "The Changing Face of Calvinism in Antwerp, 1555–1585," in *Calvinism in Europe, 1540–1620,* ed. Andrew Pettegree, Alastair Duke, and Gillian Lewis (1994; Cambridge: Cambridge University Press, reprinted 1996).

Murray, John. "Pictures of Christ." *Reformed Herald* 16:9 (February 1961).

Meyers, Jeffrey J. "Vere Homo, The Case for Pictures of Jesus: A Critical Examination of Seeing Jesus by Peter Barnes" (unpublished; Jeffrey J. Meyers, revised June 1999).

Niesel, Wilhelm. "The Witness of the Power of the Holy Spirit in the Heidelberg Catechism," (unpublished essay; 1963).

Old, Hughes Oliphant. *The Shaping of the Reformed Baptismal Rite in the Sixteenth Century* (Grand Rapids: Eerdmans, 1992).

——. *The Reading and Preaching of the Scriptures in the Worship of the Christian Church: Volume 1* (Grand Rapids: Eerdmans, 1998).

——.*The Reading and Preaching of the Scriptures in the Worship of the Christian Church: Volume 2* (Grand Rapids: Eerdmans, 1998).

Olevianus, Caspar. *A Firm Foundation,* trans. and ed. Lyle D. Bierma, Texts & Studies in Reformation & Post-Reformation Thought (Grand Rapids: Baker, 1995).

Owen, John. "Animadversions on a Treatise Entitled 'Fiat Lux,' in *The Works of John Owen,* ed. William H. Goold, 16 vols. (1965; Edinburgh: The Banner of Truth Trust,1991).

——."Sermon 15: The Chamber of Imagery in the Church of Rome Laid Open," in *The Works of John Owen,* ed. William H. Goold, 16 vols. (Edinburgh: The Banner of Truth Trust, reprinted 1991).

Perkins, William. *The Art of Prophesying with The Calling of the Ministry* (Edinburgh: The Banner of Truth Trust, revised 1996).

Postman, Neil. *Amusing Ourselves to Death: Public Discourse in the Age of Show Business* (New York: Penguin Books, 1985).

Psalter Hymnal (Grand Rapids: Christian Reformed Church, 1976).

Schaver, J. L. *The Polity of the Churches: Volume II* (3rd ed.; Chicago: Church Polity Press, 1947).

Sinnema, Donald. "The Second Sunday Service in the Early Dutch Reformed Tradition." *Calvin Theological Journal* 32 (1997): 298–333.

Spurgeon, C. H. *Lectures to My Students* (Grand Rapids: Zondervan, 1954).

The Confession of Faith, the Larger Catechism, the Shorter Catechism (Edinburgh and London: William Blackwood & Sons Ltd., 1963).

The Creeds of Christendom, ed. Philip Schaff, rev. David S. Schaff, 3 vols. (Grand Rapids: Baker, reprinted 1996).

The Psalter (rev. ed.; Grand Rapids: Eerdmans, 1965).

The Seven Ecumenical Councils of the Undivided Church, ed., Henry R. Percival, *Nicene and Post-Nicene Fathers: Second Series,* ed. Philip Schaff and Henry Wace, 14 vols. (Peabody: Hendrickson Publishers, reprinted 1994).

Turretin, Francis. *Institutes of Elenctic Theology,* trans. George Musgrave Giger, ed. James T. Dennison, Jr., 3 vols. (Phillipsburg: P&R Publishing, 1992).

Ursinus, Zacharius. *The Commentary of Dr. Zacharias Ursinus on the Heidelberg Catechism,* trans. G. W. Williard (1852; Phillipsburg: Presbyterian and Reformed, reprinted 1985).

van Baalen, Jan Karel. *The Heritage of the Fathers: A Commentary on the Heidelberg Catechism* (Grand Rapids: Eerdmans, 1948).

Van Dellen, Idzerd and Martin Monsma, *The Church Order Commentary* (Credo Books: Wyoming, MI: reprinted 2003).

VanDrunen, David M. "Celebrating Jesus' Birth–Without His Picture." *New Horizons* 27:11 (December 2006): 6–7.

——."Iconoclasm, Incarnation and Eschatology: Toward a Catholic Understanding of the Reformed Doctrine of the 'Second' Commandment." *International Journal of Systematic Theology* 6:2 (April 2004): 130–47.

Venema, Cornelis P. *But for the Grace of God: An Exposition of the Canons of Dort* (Grand Rapids: Reformed Fellowship, 1994).

Vincent, Thomas. *An Explanation of the Assembly's Shorter Catechism* (Philadelphia: Presbyterian Board of Publication, n.d.).

Watson, Thomas. *The Ten Commandments* (Edinburgh: Banner ofTruth, 1965).

Weilersbacher, Donald. "Implication of Exodus 20:3–6 for the Doctrine of Worship," in *The Biblical Doctrine of Worship*(The Reformed Presbyterian Church of North America, January 1974).

Wollebius, Johannes. *Compendium Theologiae Christianae in Reformed Dogmatics,* ed. and trans. John W. Beardslee III (Grand Rapids: Baker, 1965).

Endnotes

Introduction

1. Neil Postman, *Amusing Ourselves to Death: Public Discourse in the Age of Show Business* (New York: Penguin Books, 1985), 87

2. *Ibid.*, 116–124.

3. *Ibid.*, 121.

4. At the website, http://www.thepassionoutreach.com, quotes such as these may be found: "Perhaps the best outreach opportunity in 2000 years;" "'The Passion of the Christ' – A Lifetime of Sermons in One Movie;" "I have no doubt that the movie will be one of the greatest evangelistic tools in modern day history. I think people will go to it and then flood into the churches seeking to know the deeper implications of this movie" (Accessed June 7, 2007). Less dramatic for the 2007 movie *Evan Almighty* is the site www.arkalmighty.com.

5. Cited at http://www.csun.edu/science/health/docs/tv&health.html (Accessed May 20, 2008).

6. *The Creeds of Christendom*, ed. Philip Schaff, rev. David S. Schaff, 3 vols. (Grand Rapids: Baker, reprinted 1996), 3:586.

7. On this distinction between the hidden and revealed things of God, see Daniel R. Hyde, *God With Us: Knowing the Mystery of Who Jesus Is* (Grand Rapids: Reformation Heritage Books, 2007), 8–12.

8. This is how "The Passion Outreach" hyped the film at http://www.thepassionoutreach.com/ (Accessed May 25, 2007).

9. G. Jeffrey MacDonald, "Reformed Protestants No Longer See Images as Idolatrous." *Christianity Today* 48 (December [Web-only] 2004). Available at http://www.ctlibrary.com/ct/2004/decemberweb-only/12-6-12.0.html (Accessed May 25, 2007).

10. On the Belgic Confession see Daniel R. Hyde, *With Heart and Mouth: An Exposition of the Belgic Confession* (Grandville: Reformed Fellowship, 2008).

11. See the "Report of the 2002 Meeting of NAPARC." http://traver.org/naparc2/2002rept.htm (Accessed May 20, 2008).

12. For example, see Alastair Duke, "The Netherlands," in *The Early Reformation in Europe*, ed. Andrew Pettegree (1992; Cambridge: Cambridge University Press, reprinted 1998), 142–165; Guido Marnef, "The Changing Face of Calvinism in Antwerp, 1555–1585," in *Calvinism in Europe, 1540–1620*, ed. Andrew Pettegree, Alastair Duke, and Gillian Lewis (1994; Cambridge: Cambridge University Press, reprinted 1996), 143–159; Alastair Duke, *Reformation and Revolt in the Low Countries* (London: Hambledon and London, 2003).

13. Charles W. Baird, *The Presbyterian Liturgies: Historical Sketches* (Eugene, Oregon: Wipf & Stock Publishers, 2006), 26.

Chapter 1

1. John Calvin, *Institutes of the Christian Religion,* ed. John T. McNeill, trans. Ford Lewis Battles (Philadelphia: The Westminster Press, 1960), 1.11.8.

2. Carlos M. N. Eire *War Against the Idols: The Reformation of Worship from Erasmus to Calvin* (Cambridge: Cambridge University Press, 1986), 226.

3. Schaff, *Creeds of Christendom,* 3:398.

4. This was the interpretation of Julius Africanus (*ca.* 160–240), *Chronography* 2 in *Ante-Nicene Fathers*, ed. A. Cleveland Coxe, 10 vols. (1886; Peabody, Massachusetts: Hendrickson Publishers, Inc., reprinted 2004), 6:131. This was also the interpretation of Augustine, *City of God* 15.23–24, trans. Marcus Dods (New York; The Modern Library, 1993), 510–514. It was also supported by John Calvin, *Commentaries on the First Book of Moses Called Genesis: Volume 1*, trans. John King, Calvin's Commentaries, 22 vols. (Grand Rapids: Baker, reprinted 1996), 1:237–239.

5. This was the interpretation of Meredith G. Kline in "Divine Kingship and Son of God in Genesis 6:1–4." *Westminster Theological Journal* 24 (1962): 187–204.

6. John Calvin, *Commentaries on the Four Last Books of Moses Arranged in the Form of a Harmony: Volume Third*, trans. Charles William Bingham, Calvin's Commentaries 22 vols. (Grand Rapids: Baker, reprinted 1996), 3:330 cf. *Institutes*, 1.11.8.

7. John Calvin, *Commentaries on the Four Last Books of Moses Arranged in the Form of a Harmony: Volume Third*, trans. Charles William Bingham, Calvin's Commentaries 22 vols. (Grand Rapids: Baker, reprinted 1996), 3:330–331.

8. Schaff, *Creeds*, 3:342.

9. Calvin, *Institutes*, 1.11.8.

10. Postman, *Amusing Ourselves to Death*, 9.

11. Michael S. Horton, *Lord and Servant: A Covenant Christology* (Louisville: Westminster John Knox Press, 2005), 63.

12. On how Deuteronomy 4 and other Old Testament texts recount the history of salvation to various audiences and generations, see Paul R. House, "Examining the narrative of Old Testament Narrative: An Exploration in Biblical Theology." *Westminster Theological Journal* 67:2 (Fall 2005): 229–245.

13. David VanDrunen, "Iconoclasm, Incarnation and Eschatology: Toward a Catholic Understanding of the Reformed Doctrine of the 'Second' Commandment." *International Journal of Systematic Theology* 6:2 (April 2004): 130–147. For a popular form of this article see David M. VanDrunen, "Celebrating Jesus' Birth–Without His Picture." *New Horizons* 27:11 (December 2006): 6–7. An example of the traditional appeal to this text is John Owen, "Animadversions on a Treatise Entitled 'Fiat Lux,' in *The Works of John Owen*, ed. William H. Goold, 16 vols. (1965; Edinburgh: The Banner of Truth Trust, 1991), 14:126.

14. VanDrunen, "Iconoclasm, Incarnation and Eschatology," 134.

15. *Ibid.*, 136.

16. Cited in Calvin, *Institutes,* 1.11.4

17. *Ibid.*, 1.11.1, 2.

18. On this, see Robert Grigg, "Aniconic Worship and the Apologetic Tradition: A Note on Canon 36 of the Council of Elvira." *Church History* 45.4 (December 1976): 428–433.

19. *picturas in ecclesia esse non debere, ne quod colitur et adoratur in parietibus depingatur*; Grigg, "Aniconic Worship," 429.

20. *Ibid.*, 431–432.

21. Jeffrey J. Meyers, "*Vere Homo,* The Case *for* Pictures of Jesus: A Critical Examination of *Seeing Jesus* by Peter Barnes" (Jeffrey J. Meyers, revised June 1999), 22.

22. *Ibid.*, 27, 28.

23. *Ibid.*, 37.

24. *Ibid.*, 34.

25. John Murray, "Pictures of Christ." *Reformed Herald* 16:9 (February 1961): 66.

26. For an exposition of the Incarnation see Hyde, *God With Us.*

27. Schaff, *Creeds,* 3:403.

28. As exemplified in St. John Damascene, *On Holy Images* (London: Thomas Baker, 1898).

29. As found at: http://www.alliancenet.org/CC/article/0,,PTID23682%7CCHID 125099%7CCIID1712182,00.html (Cited June 7, 2008).

30. John Frame, *The Doctrine of the Christian Life* (Phillipsburg: P&R, 2008), 484–86.

31. Peter Barnes, *Seeing Jesus: The Case Against Pictures of Our Lord Jesus Christ* (Edinburgh: Banner of Truth Trust, 1990), 1.

32. VanDrunen, "Iconoclasm, Incarnation and Eschatology," 139. See the contrary position put forth by John M. Frame, *The Doctrine of the Christian Life*, 484–86. Frame argues that because we *do know* that Jesus was male, around thirty years old when he ministered, and was Semitic, that we can therefore image him for art or educational purposes.

33. VanDrunen, *"Iconoclasm, Incarnation, and Eschatology,"* 140, 141.

34. Barnes, *Seeing Jesus*, 2.

35. Schaff, *Creeds*, 3:687.

36. As found at http://books.google.com/books?id=Zjs3AAAAMAAJ (Accessed May 21, 2008).

37. Loraine Boettner, *Roman Catholicism* (Philadelphia: The Presbyterian and Reformed Publishing Company, 1962), 284.

38. Edward M. Curtis "The Theological Basis for the Prohibition of Images in the Old Testament." *Journal of the Evangelical Theological Society* 28:3 (September 1985): 281.

39. Along with this standard argument against images based on the reality of the Incarnation, many Reformed authors use the argument that because of the Incarnation we cannot make images because Christ now has two natures and is Immanuel, the God-man. On this, see Thomas Watson, *The Ten Commandments* (Edinburgh: Banner of Truth, 1965), 62; Thomas Vincent, *An Explanation of the Assembly's Shorter Catechism* (Philadelphia: Presbyterian Board of Publication, n.d.), 162; Ralph Erskine, *Faith No Fancy: Or, a Treatise of Mental Images* (Philadelphia: William M'Culloch, 1805), 51; James Durham, *The Law Unsealed: or, A Practical Exposition of the Ten Commandments. With a Resolution of Several Momentous Questions and Cases of Conscience* (Edinburgh: D. Schaw, 1802), 64, 68.

40. On the *sursum corda* see Daniel R. Hyde, "Lift Up Your Hearts: Increasing the Use of the *Sursum Corda.*" *Reformed Worship* 82 (December 2006): 33–35.

41. VanDrunen, "Iconoclasm, Incarnation and Eschatology," 144.

42. *Ibid.*, 145.

43. Meyers, "*Vere Homo*, 1.

44. *Ibid.*, 4–5 n4. This claim may be answered by reading the following Reformation treatises specifically against images: Andreas Karlstadt, *On the Removal of Images* (1522) in *A Reformation Debate: Karlstadt, Emser, and Eck on Sacred Images: Three Treatises in Translation*, trans. By Bryan D. Mangrum, Giuseppe Scavizzi, Renaissance and Reformation Texts in Translation 5 (2nd edition; Toronto: Centre for Reformation and Renaissance Studies, 1998); Martin Bucer, *That Any Kind of Images May Not Be Permitted* (1530), which was soon translated into English as *A Treatise Declaring and Showing that Images are Not to be Suffered in Churches*, trans. W. Marshall (W. Marshall, 1535); Ulrich Zwingli, *Commentary on True and False Religion* (1525), which may be read under the same title, ed. Samuel Macauley Jackson (Durham: The Labyrinth Press, 1981). On these and other writings see Carlos M. N. Eire, *War Against the Idols: The Reformation of Worship from Erasmus to Calvin* (Cambridge: Cambridge University Press, 1989) and Lee Palmer Wandel, *Voracious Idols and Violent Hands: Iconoclasm in Reformation Zurich, Strasbourg, and Basel* (Cambridge: Cambridge University Press, 1999).

45. *Psalter Hymnal* (Grand Rapids: Christian Reformed Church, 1976), 7.

46. These questions and answered are found in Schaff, *Creeds*, 3:343.

47. See also the Westminster Shorter Catechism, which exposits the second commandment in terms of worshipping God as he requires in his Word (Q&A 50–52); Schaff, *Creeds*, 3:687.

48. Calvin, *Last Four Books of Moses: Volume Second,* 2:108. Cf. Calvin, *Institutes*, 1.11.9; *Catechism of the Church of Geneva*, Q&A 146, in *Selected Works of John Calvin: Tracts and Letters: Volume 1,* ed. Henry Beveridge and Jules Bonnet, 7 vols. (Grand Rapids: Baker, 1983), 2:58; Heinrich Bullinger, *The Decades of Henry Bullinger*, ed. Thomas Harding, 2 vols. (Grand Rapids: Reformation Heritage Books, 2004), 1:223–232; Johannes Wollebius, *Compendium Theologiae Christianae in Reformed Dogmatics*, ed. and trans. John W. Beardslee III (Grand Rapids: Baker, 1965), 206.

49. Francis Turretin, *Institutes of Elenctic Theology*, trans. George Musgrave Giger, ed. James T. Dennison, Jr., 3 vols. (Phillipsburg: P&R Publishing, 1992), 2:62, 63, 65.

50. Cf. the discussion of Acts 17 above.

51. In *An Introduction to the Heidelberg Catechism*, ed. Lyle D. Bierma, Texts & Studies in Reformation & Post-Reformation Thought (Grand Rapids: Baker, 2005), 157.

52. *Ibid.*, 193 cf. Q&A 169 on page 194.

53. Calvin, *Institutes*, 1.11.12.

54. *Register of the Epistles of Saint Gregory the Great* 9.105, trans. James Barmby, in *Nicene and Post-Nicene Fathers: Second Series,* ed. Philip Schaff and Henry Wace, 14 vols. (Peabody, Massachusetts: Hendrickson Publishers, Inc., reprinted 2004), 13:23.

55. *Ibid., Epistle* 11.13, 13:53–54. Cf. Calvin's comments on Gregory's dictum that images were the books of the laity in *Institutes*, 1.11.5, 7.

56. Wilhemus a'Brakel, *The Christian's Reasonable Service*, trans. Bartel Elshout, 4 vols. (Ligonier, PA: Soli Deo Gloria Publications, 1992), 3:108, 109, 110.

57. Meyers, "*Vere Homo,*" 7–8.

58. *Ibid.*, 62.

59. On the Incarnation, see Hyde, *God With Us* .

60. Schaff, *Creeds*, 3:836.

61. *Ibid.*, 3:836–37.

62. *Ibid.*, 3:837.

63. Meyers, "*Vere Homo,*" 73.

64. Schaff, *Creeds*, 3:837.

65. *Ibid.*, 3:837.

66. Jerome, *Letter* 51.9, trans. W. H. Fremantle, G. Lewis, and W. G. Martley, in *Nicene and Post-Nicene Fathers: Second Series*, 14 vols. (1893; Peabody, Massachusetts: Hendrickson Publishers, Inc., reprinted 2004), 6:88–89.

67. *Against Heresies* 1.25.6, in *Ante-Nicene Fathers*, ed. Alexander Roberts and James Donaldson, 10 vols. (1885; Peabody, Massachusetts: Hendrickson Publishers, Inc., reprinted 2004), 1:351.

68. *The Confession of Faith, the Larger Catechism, the Shorter Catechism* (Edinburgh and London: William Blackwood & Sons Ltd., 1963), 79–80.

69. On the clause in Q&A 109 that we are forbidden to make inward images, and the debate among eighteenth and nineteenth-century Scottish Presbyterians, see John K. LaShell, "Imagination and Idol: A Puritan Tension." *Westminster Theological Journal* 49:2 (1987): 305–334.

70. Meyers, "*Vere Homo,*" 75.

71. Donald Weilersbacher, "Implication of Exodus 20:3–6 for the Doctrine of Worship," in *The Biblical Doctrine of Worship* (The **Reformed** Presbyterian Church of North America, January 1974), 22.

72. Meyers, "*Vere Homo,*" 13. Meyers accuses Barnes of conflating worship, art, and education, and thus distinguishing the issue of making images as well as worshipping images in Meyers, "*Vere Homo,*" 17, 39, but this is the Reformed interpretation of the second commandment as the confessions and catechisms have shown. Cf. Chuck Baynard, *Teaching Classic Reformed Theology in the 21st Century, Teacher's Manual: The Second Helvetic Confession* (n.d.), 31–37. Found at http://www.christianobserver.org/Files/helvetic.pdf (Accessed June 8, 2007).

73. Calvin, *Four Last Books of Moses: Volume Second*, 2:108.

Chapter 2

1. Schaff, *Creeds*, 3:343.

2. John Calvin, "An Admonition, Showing the Advantage Which Christendom Might Derive From an Inventory of Relics," ed. and trans. Henry Beveridge, in *Selected Works of John Calvin, Tracts and Letters: Volume 1*, ed. Henry Beveridge and Jules Bonnet, 7 vols. (Grand Rapids: Baker, 1983), 1:289. Cf. Calvin, *Institutes*, 1.11.7.

3. Schaff, *Creed*

4. John Dod, *A Plaine and Familiar Exposition of the Tenne Commandements*, (London,1604), 58.

5. On the second commandment and its relation to preaching, see Michael S. Horton, *The Law of Perfect Freedom* (Chicago: Moody Press, 1993), 71–94.

6. Schaff, *Creeds*, 3:402.

7. St. Augustine, *A Harmony of the Gospels* 10.16, trans. S. D. F. Salmond, ed. M. B. Riddle, in *Nicene and Post-Nicene Fathers: First Series*, 14 vols. (1888; Peabody, Massachusetts: Hendrickson Publishers, Inc., reprinted 2004), 6:83.

8. John Owen, "Sermon 15: The Chamber of Imagery in the Church of Rome Laid Open," in *The Works of John Owen*, ed. William H. Goold, 16 vols. (Edinburgh: The Banner of Truth Trust, reprinted 1991), 8:554.

9. This language of "tourists" and "seekers" comes from Michael S. Horton, "Seekers or Tourists?: Or the Difference Between Pilgrimage and Vacation." *Modern Reformation* 10:4 (July/August 2001): 12–18; Cf. "How the Kingdom Comes." *Christianity Today* 50:1 (January 2006): 42.

10. Calvin, *Institutes*, 4.1.5.

11. William Perkins, *The Art of Prophesying with The Calling of the Ministry* (Edinburgh: The Banner of Truth Trust, revised 1996), 86.

12. John Chrysostom, *Commentary on Galatians*, rev. Gross Alexander, in *Nicene and Post-Nicene Fathers: First Series*, ed. Philip Schaff, 14 vols. (1889; Peabody, Massachusetts: Hendrickson Publishers, Inc., reprinted 2004), 13:24.

13. Martin Luther, *Commentary on Galatians*, trans. Erasmus Middleton, ed. John Prince Fallowes (Grand Rapids: Kregel Classics, 1979), 107.

14. Calvin, *Institutes*, 1.11.7.

15. John Calvin, *Commentaries on the Epistle to the Galatians*, trans. William Pringle, Calvin's Commentaries, 22 vols. (Grand Rapids: Baker, reprinted 1996), 21:79, 80–81.

16. John Calvin, *Sermons on Galatians* (Audubon, New Jersey: Old Paths Publications, 1995), 320.

17. Turretin, *Institutes of Elenctic Theology*, 2:61.

18. Schaff, *Creeds*, 3:328.

19. E.g., Calvin, *Institutes*, 1.9.1, 3 cf. 4.8.13.

20. Wilhelm Niesel, "The Witness of the Power of the Holy Spirit in the Heidelberg Catechism," (unpublished essay; 1963): 9, 10.

21. Daniel R. Hyde, "The Holy Spirit in the Heidelberg Catechism." *Mid-America Journal of Theology* 17 (2006): 222–223.

22. Eugene P. Heideman, "God the Holy Spirit," in *Guilt, Grace, and Gratitude: A Commentary on the Heidelberg Catechism*, ed. Donald J. Bruggink (New York: The Half Moon Press, 1963), 118.

23. Olevianus, *De substantia*, 2.33, cited in R. Scott Clark, *Caspar Olevian and the Substance of the Covenant: The Double Benefit of Christ*, Rutherford Studies in Historical Theology (Edinburgh: Rutherford House, 2005), 192.

24. *De substantia*, 2.51, cited in Clark, *Caspar Olevian and the Substance of the Covenant*, 193.

25. Caspar Olevianus, *A Firm Foundation*, trans. and ed. Lyle D. Bierma, Texts & Studies in Reformation & Post-Reformation Thought (Grand Rapids: Baker, 1995), 11.

26. Zacharius Ursinus, *The Commentary of Dr. Zacharias Ursinus on the Heidelberg Catechism*, trans. G. W. Williard (1852; Phillipsburg: Presbyterian and Reformed, reprinted 1985), 112.

27. Schaff, *Creeds*, 3:328–329.

28. *Ibid.*, 3:337

29. *Ibid.*, 3:337.

30. *Ibid.*, 3:343.

31. *Ibid.*, 3:832.

32. C. H. Spurgeon, *Lectures to My Students* (Grand Rapids: Zondervan, 1954), 75–76.

33. Schaff, *Creeds*, 3:345.

34. On the development of catechetical preaching and its relation to the Didache see Hughes Oliphant Old, *The Reading and Preaching of the Scriptures in the Worship of the Christian Church: Volume 1* (Grand Rapids: Eerdmans, 1998), 255–65.

35. See the commentary on these sermons in Hughes Oliphant Old, *The Reading and Preaching of the Scriptures in the Worship of the Christian Church: Volume 2* (Grand Rapids: Eerdmans, 1998), 5–18.

36. *Ibid.*, 196–202.

37. *Ibid.*, 224–228.

38. *Ibid.*, 382–385

39. For an extensive history, see Donald Sinnema, "The Second Sunday Service in the Early Dutch Reformed Tradition." *Calvin Theological Journal* 32 (1997): 298–333.

40. As translated in *The Psalter* (rev. ed.; Grand Rapids: Eerdmans, 1965), 187.

41. As cited in Jan Karel van Baalen, *The Heritage of the Fathers: A Commentary on the Heidelberg Catechism* (Grand Rapids: Eerdmans, 1948), 25.

42. As cited in Idzerd Van Dellen and Martin Monsma, *The Church Order Commentary* (Credo Books: Wyoming, MI: reprinted 2003), 279.

43. J.L. Schaver, *The Polity of the Churches: Volume II* (3rd ed.; Chicago: Church Polity Press, 1947), 159.

44. *Ibid.*, 159.

45. See the excellent chapter by Cornelis P. Venema entitled, "The Canons of Dort and Reformed Evangelism," in *But for the Grace of God: An Exposition of the Canons of Dort* (Grand Rapids: Reformed Fellowship, 1994), 83–93.

46. For a list of delegates, see *Crisis in the Reformed Churches*, ed. Peter Y. De Jong (Grand Rapids: Reformed Fellowship, Inc., 2008), 213–21.

47. Schaff, *Creeds*, 3:581.

48. *Ibid.*, 3:581.

49. *Ibid.*, 3:582.

50. Anthony Hoekema, "The Missionary Focus of the Canons of Dort," *Calvin Theological Journal* (November 1972): 212.

51. *Ibid.*, 210–11.

52. See Venema, *But for the Grace of God*, 68–69.

53. Schaff, *Creeds*, 3:588–89.

54. *Ibid.*, 3:589.

55. *Ibid.*, 3:590.

56. *Ibid.*, 3:590.

57. *Ibid.*, 3:590.

58. *Ibid.*, 3:592.

59. *Ibid.*, 3:594.

60. *Ibid.*, 3:595.

61. *Ibid.*, 3:594.

Chapter 3

1. Schaff, *Creeds,* 3:424.

2. The Seven Ecumenical Councils of the Undivided Church, ed., Henry R. Percival, Nicene and Post-Nicene Fathers: Second Series, ed. Philip Schaff and Henry Wace, 14 vols. (Peabody: Hendrickson Publishers, reprinted 1994), 14:544. For the response of the iconodules at the Council of Nicea II in 787, see 14:549–51.

3. On the history and theology of these errors, see Hyde, *God With Us,* 29–40, 77–87.

4. *Ibid.*, 55.

5. VanDrunen, "Iconoclasm, Incarnation and Eschatology," 147 n42.

6. Calvin, *Institutes*, 1.11.13.

7. *Luther's Large Catechism: A Contemporary Translation with Study Questions*, trans. and ed. F. Samuel Janzow (Saint Louis: Concordia Publishing House, 1978), 107.

8. *Ibid.*, 104, 109.

9. *Psalter Hymnal,* 132.

10. Schaff, *Creeds,* 3:424.

11. "Baptism of Infants: Form Number 1" in *Ibid.*, 123.

12. *Ibid.*, 123.

13. Schaff, *Creeds*, 3:425.

14. Calvin, *Institutes,* 4.15.1; cf. Wollebius, *Compendium Theologiae Christianae,* 23.1.13; M. J. Bosma, *Exposition of Reformed Doctrine* (4th ed.; Grand Rapids: Smitter Book Company, 1927), 258–9.

15. Francis Turretin, *Institutes of Elenctic Theology*, trans. George Musgrave Giger, ed. James T. Dennison, Jr., 3 vols. (Phillipsburg: P&R, 1997), 3:19.11.2.5. Herman Bavinck described the two sacraments as incorporation (baptism) and maturation (communion) in Herman Bavinck, *Our Reasonable Faith*, trans. Henry Zylstra (Grand Rapids: Eerdmans, 1956), 542.

16. Hyde, *With Heart and Mouth*, 452–53 cf. Daniel R. Hyde, "We Confess: Article 34." *The Outlook* 56:6 (June 2006): 10.

17. Schaff, *Creeds,* 3:427.

18. *Institutes,* 4.15.11.

19. *Ibid.,* 4.15.3.

20. Cited in Hughes Oliphant Old, *The Shaping of the Reformed Baptismal Rite in the Sixteenth Century* (Grand Rapids: Eerdmans, 1992), 211.

21. *Ibid.*, 211.

22. *Ibid.*, 207.

23. *The Confession of Faith*, 101.

24. *Institutes*, 4.18.11.

25. On the Lord's Supper, see Hyde, *With Heart and Mouth,* 463–76 cf. Daniel R. Hyde, "We Confess: Article 35." *The Outlook* 56:7 (July/August 2006): 12–15.

26. *Luther's Works, Volume 38: Word and Sacrament IV*, ed. Jaroslav Jan Pelikan, Hilton C. Oswald and Helmut T. Lehmann (1971; Philadelphia: Fortress Press, reprinted 1999), 38:87.

27. Schaff, *Creeds*, 3:428.

28. *Ibid.*, 3:429.

29. *Ibid.*, 3:429–30.

30. *The Letters of Saint Athanasius Concerning the Holy Spirit*, trans. C. R. B. Shapland (New York: The Philosophical Library, 1951), book 1.

31. Schaff, *Creeds*, 3:431.

32. *The Confession of Faith*, 104.

Note to the Reader

The publisher invites you to respond to us about this book by writing Reformed Fellowship, Inc., 3363 Hickory Ridge Ct. SW, Grandville, MI 49418, USA. You may also email us at president@reformedfellowship.net

Founded in 1951, Reformed Fellowship, Inc., is a religious and strictly non-profit organization composed of a group of Christian believers who hold to the biblical Reformed faith. Our purpose is to advocate and propagate this faith, to nurture those who seek to live in obedience to it, to give sharpened expression to it, to stimulate the doctrinal sensitivities of those who profess it, to promote the spiritual welfare and purity of the Reformed churches, and to encourage Christian action.

Members of Reformed Fellowship express their adherence to the Calvinistic creeds as formulated in the Belgic Confession, the Heidelberg Catechism, the Canons of Dort, and the Westminster Confession and Catechisms.

To fulfill our mission, we publish a monthly journal, *The Outlook*, and we publish books and Bible study guides. Our website is **www.reformedfellowship.net**